Aviation Weather Laboratory Manual

By Peter F. Lester

ISBN-13: 978-0-88487-447-8
ISBN-10: 0-88487-447-8

Jeppesen
55 Inverness Drive East
Englewood, CO 80112-5498
Web Site: www.jeppesen.com
Email: Captain@jeppesen.com
Copyright © Jeppesen
All Rights Reserved. Published 1998, 2001, 2007
Printed in the United States of America

10001788-002

TABLE OF CONTENTS

INTRODUCTION

BACKGROUND

The *Aviation Weather Laboratory Manual* is designed as a companion to *Aviation Weather, 3rd Edition*. Its purpose is to expand and enhance the material in that textbook with some practical exercises and problems. The Laboratory Manual draws heavily from the textbook for background information. Material about weather reports, forecasts, and charts is integrated into various chapters and Appendix D of the textbook. Appendix D was compiled from the FAA Advisory Circular *AC 00-45F, Aviation Weather Services,* and related publications. Therefore, all information necessary to complete the exercises is contained in this Laboratory Manual and the textbook. Each exercise includes specific references to chapters and appendices of *Aviation Weather, 3rd Edition*. Should you wish to do supplementary reading, references are also given to related sections in *Aviation Weather Services*.

STRUCTURE OF THE LABORATORY MANUAL

The Manual consists of 17 exercises that generally parallel the chapters in the textbook. Table 1 lists each exercise and the corresponding primary *Aviation Weather* chapter and/or appendix. You will notice that there are some exercises without chapter references. Exercises 8 and 13 provide tools for the use and interpretation of meteorological charts and data that are used in later exercises. Specific exercises for Chapters 10 and 15 in *Aviation Weather* are not included in the Manual.

STRUCTURE OF THE EXERCISES

Each exercise follows a specific four-section structure.

Objectives: A short list of the specific goals of the exercise. Includes a reference list of the chapters and appendices in *Aviation Weather* related to the exercise.

Background: An overview of the material in the exercise with occasional added information that expands the references.

Tasks: The exercise assignments.

Questions: A series of problems designed to review, enhance, or integrate the results of the exercise.

Important material in the *Laboratory Manual* is highlighted in blue to facilitate completion of exercises and later review. Highlighted material includes figure captions, some otherwise difficult-to-find data on maps and charts, as well as definitions of terms and important concepts. The pages are perforated to allow you to tear them out for checking by your instructor. This lets you continue working on the next exercise. Pages also are three-hole drilled so the manual can be placed in a loose leaf binder and pages previously removed for grading can be replaced after they are returned. This will allow the completed manual to be retained in an organized fashion for future reference.

USING REAL-TIME WEATHER INFOMATION

Your understanding and use of aviation weather information can be enhanced by your exposure to weather information beyond that found in the Laboratory Manual. By following day-to-day changes in weather conditions across your flying area or across the globe, you will become familiar with the size, intensity, impact, and timing of weather systems. Also, the exercises will help you become knowledgeable about weather observation and forecasts and their presentation in alphanumeric and graphical formats.

The formats of all alphanumeric data (reports, forecasts, etc.) used in this Laboratory Manual are identical with those being used operationally in 2007. However, weather map graphics used here are only a sample of what is available. (e.g., see examples in *Aviation Weather, 3rd Edition* and in *AC 00-45F*). For instructional purposes, maps for the following exercises were chosen for their clarity and for the detail of the plotted data and the analyses.

Regular practice in acquiring and interpreting weather information in a wide variety of formats outside of the exercises is essential for developing your capability and confidence to make the best use of that information.

CAUTION: The distribution of weather information via the Internet is not considered an operational delivery mechanism by NWS. internet sites or some of their products are often experimental and there is no guarantee that you will have access to the latest or most accurate information. Official sources should be used for flight planning (see *Aviation Weather*, Chapter 16).

EXERCISE 1:

THE INTERNATIONAL STANDARD ATMOSPHERE (ISA)

OBJECTIVES:

- To reinforce your background knowledge of the properties and the vertical structure of the earth's atmosphere

- To familiarize you with the format and common nomenclature of atmospheric soundings, with special attention given to the International Standard Atmosphere (ISA)

Reference: *Aviation Weather*, Chapter 1, "The Atmosphere" and Appendix B, "Standard Atmosphere."

BACKGROUND DISCUSSION:

Your textbook describes the composition, properties, and vertical structure of the atmosphere in some detail. This exercise is designed to emphasize, reinforce, and clarify some of the most important aspects of that description. You will perform a series of tasks designed to familiarize you with the International Standard Atmosphere (ISA). (Figure 1-1) The importance of ISA cannot be stressed enough. It is an extremely useful model that gives you typical values of pressure, temperature, and density as a function of altitude. ISA will serve you in several ways: as a reference for comparison with actual conditions; as a memory device for recalling the nomenclature and the structure of the atmosphere; and as a learning tool in your introduction to the meaning and application of atmospheric soundings. ISA is also used extensively in aircraft and instrument design. However, you must realize that ISA is only a "model," it does not give an instantaneous state of the vertical structure of the atmosphere. Rather it approximates actual conditions with an annual average of the atmosphere in middle latitudes. In the current exercise, you will familiarize yourself with the vertical distributions of temperature, pressure, mass, and oxygen by doing some simple calculations with ISA. You will then compare the ISA temperature sounding with average temperature soundings from the polar and tropical regions to illustrate variations to be expected across the globe. Finally, to summarize your work on ISA, you will answer a series of questions based on both your textbook reading and this exercise.

TASK 1-1: AVERAGE VERTICAL TEMPERATURE STRUCTURE.

In figure 1-1, locate and label the following layers and boundaries: Stratopause, Troposphere, Mesosphere, Tropopause, Stratosphere. Note that the Thermosphere and the Mesopause have been identified in the diagram.

TASK 1-2: ATMOSPHERIC PRESSURE AND MASS.

Atmospheric pressure is a measure of the weight of the atmosphere per a unit area, at the level of measurement. For example, at sea level, the standard atmosphere exerts a pressure of 14.7 pounds per square inch (1013.2mb). At 20,000 feet, it exerts a pressure of 6.8 pounds per square inch (466mb). Since gravity varies only slightly through the depth of the lower atmosphere, we can state this in another way: **atmospheric pressure at a given altitude is directly proportional to the mass of the atmosphere above that altitude**.

1. Use the ISA altitude and pressure data in Appendix B of *Aviation Weather* and table 1-1 below to interpolate the pressures and altitudes above which the specified percentage of atmospheric mass is found. For example, in table 1-1, 50% of the mass will be above the level at which the pressure decreases to one-half of its sea level value.

TABLE 1-1

Mass	Pressure (mb)	Altitude (ft, MSL)
100% above	1013.25	0
90% above		
75% above		
50% above		506.6
25% above		
10% above		

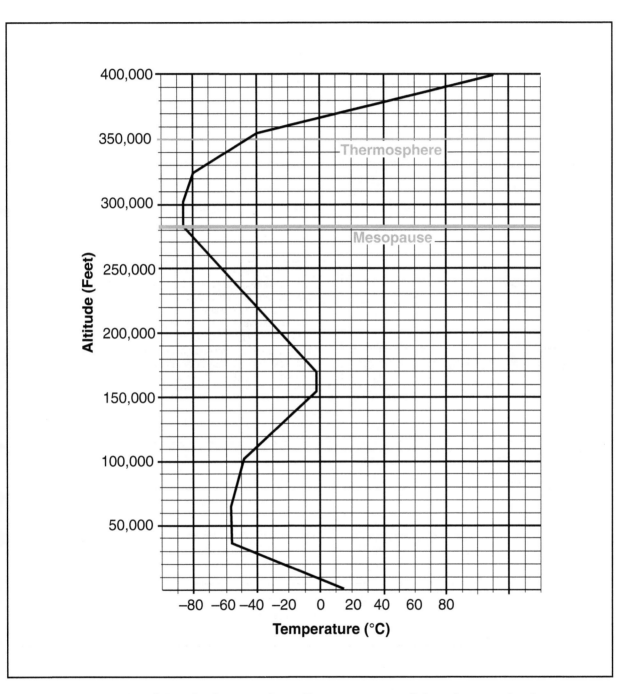

Figure 1-1. International Standard Atmosphere. Temperature conditions from sea level to 400,000 feet MSL.

2. Figure 1-2 shows the lower part of the ISA where most aircraft fly. Use the percentage scale at the top of figure 1-2 to plot the mass (%) as a function of the altitudes that you have written in table 1-1.

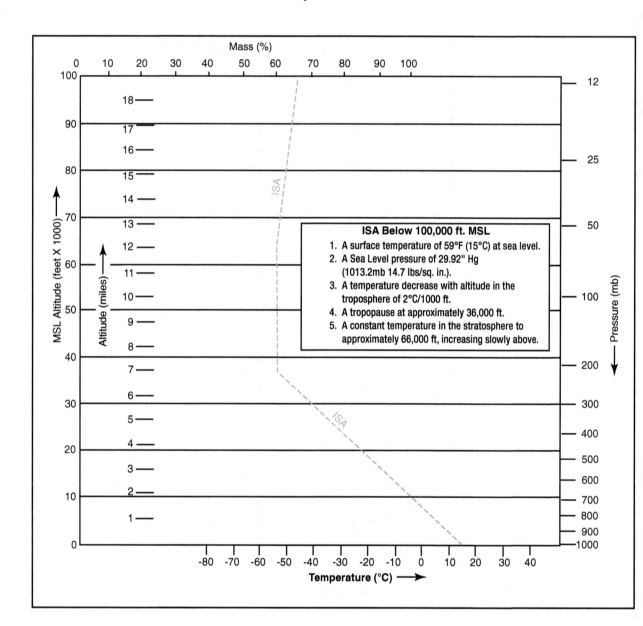

Figure 1-2. ISA Temperature Sounding. Vertical axis is labeled with altitude (left) and pressure (right). Horizontal axis is labeled with temperature (bottom) and mass (%) at the top.

NAME: _____

DATE: _____ CLASS: _____

TASK 1-3: ALTITUDE, PRESSURE, AND OXYGEN.

The amount of oxygen available for breathing decreases with height in proportion to the total pressure of the atmosphere, at least in the lowest few hundred thousand feet. The altitudes given below are critical for the use of supplemental oxygen in an unpressurized aircraft. Put the answers to the following questions in table 1-2.

1. What is the atmospheric pressure (mb) at each altitude? (Interpolate from figure 1-2)

2. What is the approximate ratio of the amount of oxygen, at each level, to the amount of oxygen at sea level? (Hint: express the ratio of each pressure to sea level pressure as a percentage.)

3. What is the rule for the use of supplemental oxygen at each level? (Review *Aviation Weather,* Chapter 1)

4. Use a straight edge and a red pencil to draw horizontal lines on figures 1-1 and 1-2 at the critical altitudes listed in table 1-2.

TABLE 1-2

Altitude (ft, MSL)	1 (mb)	2 (%)	3 (Rule)
5,000	843.6	83	Supplemental oxygen recommended above 5,000 feet at night.
10,000	_____	_____	_____
12,500	_____	_____	_____
14,000	_____	_____	_____
40,000	_____	_____	_____
50,000	_____	_____	_____
63,000	_____	_____	_____

TASK 1-4: DEVIATIONS FROM ISA.

Since many aircraft instruments are referenced to ISA, they will have some errors when the actual conditions deviate from ISA. These errors are often predictable and can be compensated for if the non-standard conditions are known. This problem gives you an example of some of the deviations that can occur. Figure 1-3 shows average soundings from tropical and polar regions along with the ISA sounding.

1. Indicate the tropopause in each sounding of figure 1-3 by drawing a short, horizontal red line between the troposphere and stratosphere. Label the line with a "T" for tropopause. What is the range of tropopause altitudes?

    Polar _____feet to Tropical _____feet

2. In figure 1-3, shade the area between the ISA sounding curve and the other two sounding curves. Use blue if the sounding is colder than ISA and red if it is warmer.

3. Compute the temperature differences between ISA and the other two soundings at the altitudes listed in table 1-3. Compute the temperature difference as shown in table 1-3. The difference will be positive if the temperature is warmer than ISA and negative if it is colder.

4. Do you notice any changes in the relationship of the three soundings (polar, tropical, and ISA) from the troposphere to the stratosphere? If so, describe them.

TABLE 1-3

TEMPERATURE DEVIATION $(T_{sounding} - T_{ISA})$ $C°$

Altitude	Average Polar Sounding	Average Tropical Sounding
Sea Level	_____	_____
10,000 ft	_____	_____
30,000 ft	_____	_____
60,000 ft	_____	_____

NAME: _____

DATE: _____ CLASS: _____

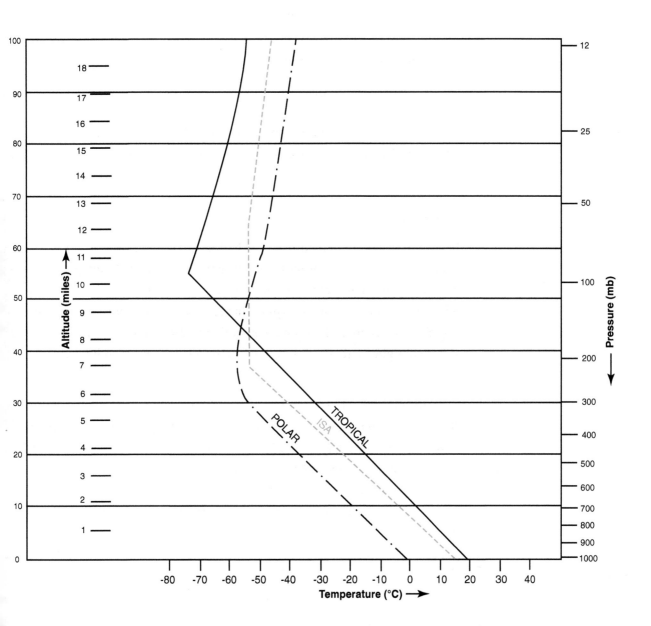

Figure 1-3. Average Soundings. Average tropical and polar soundings and ISA temperature conditions for the troposphere and lower stratosphere.

TASK 1-5: LAPSE RATE.

A temperature sounding is not only characterized by the actual temperature values, but also by the rate at which the temperature changes as altitude increases. That rate of change is known as the "temperature lapse rate" or simply lapse rate (LR). By definition, LR is given by

$$LR = (T_{lower} - T_{upper})/DELZ,$$

where T_{lower} is the temperature at the bottom of a layer, T_{upper} is the temperature at the top, and DELZ is the thickness of the layer. LR is illustrated in figure 1-4. **Note:** If lapse rate is positive, temperature decreases with height. If lapse rate is zero, temperature **does not change** with height (isothermal). If lapse rate is negative, temperature increases with height (inversion).

1. Label the unambiguous portions of the ISA sounding in figure 1-1 as "Positive," "Zero (Isothermal)," or "Negative (Inversion)." Notice that the boundaries of each layer you identified in Task 1 are located at altitudes where lapse rates change sharply. This is, in fact, how those layers were initially classified. In later chapters and exercises, you will learn about the significant effects that different temperature lapse rates can have on weather.

2. The lapse rates for the ISA are constant in the troposphere and lower stratosphere; that is, when plotted on linear graph paper, they are straight lines. Compute the lapse rates for the troposphere (0 to 30,000 feet MSL) and lower stratosphere (40,000 to 50,000 feet MSL) by using the information in figure 1-2 and completing table 1-4. **Note:** Altitudes must be expressed in 1,000's of feet (Kft) for the answers to be in familiar units (C° per 1,000 feet).

TABLE 1-4
ISA LAPSE RATE COMPUTATION
(INTERPOLATE FROM FIGURE 1-2)

Troposphere		Stratosphere	
T_{lower} _____ °C	Z_{lower} __0__ Kft	T_{lower} _____°C	Z_{lower} __40__ Kft
T_{upper} _____ °C	Z_{upper} __30__ Kft	T_{upper} _____°C	Z_{upper} __50__ Kft
$(T_{lower} - T_{upper})$ _____°C	DELZ _____ Kft	$(T_{lower} - T_{upper})$ _____ °C	DELZ _____ Kft
$LR = (T_{lower} - T_{upper})/DELZ =$ _____ C°/1,000 ft		$LR = (T_{lower} - T_{upper})/DELZ =$ _____ C°/1,000 ft	

NAME: _____

DATE: _____ CLASS: _____

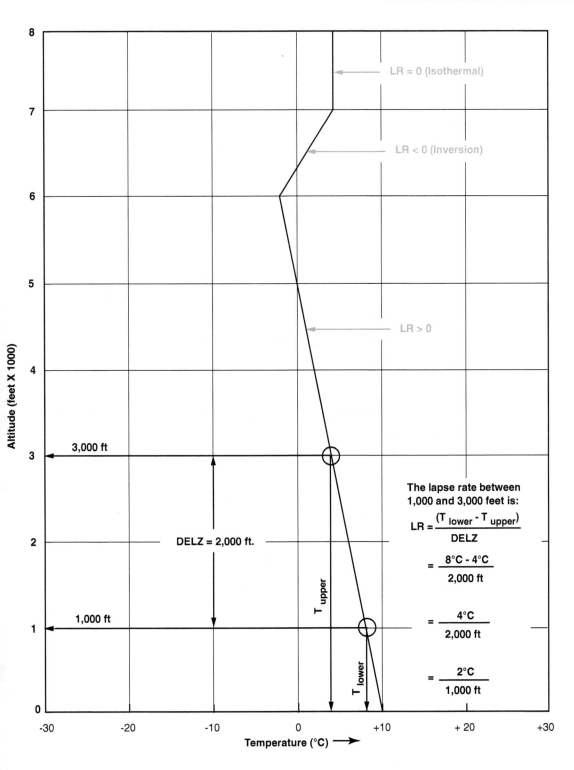

Figure 1-4. Lapse Rates. Lower tropospheric sounding showing the general method for the computation of lapse rate (LR) and examples of positive, zero (isothermal), and negative (inversion) lapse rates.

QUESTIONS

1. The sea level temperature in ISA is 15°C. The lapse rate of ISA in the troposphere is _____ C°/1,000 feet. (See task 1-5, number 2.) The tropopause height in ISA is _____ feet. Based on these numbers, compute the tropopause temperature: _____°C. Show your work below. Compare your result with figure 1-3 of this exercise and Appendix B in *Aviation Weather*.

2. The atmospheric layer in figure 1-1 with the majority of clouds and precipitation is _____. Approximately what percentage of the atmosphere's mass is found in that layer? _____%

3. If you fly your aircraft to an altitude of 1,500 feet MSL, the atmospheric pressure will be about _____ inches of mercury (_____ mb) less than it is at sea level.

4. Do you see any relationship between the deviation of tropospheric temperatures from ISA values and the MSL altitude of the tropopause in figure 1-3? Describe the relationship.

EXERCISE 2:

ATMOSPHERIC ENERGY AND TEMPERATURE

OBJECTIVES:

- To examine some characteristics and effects of sun-earth geometry
- To introduce elementary weather map analysis
- To become familiar with the use of various temperature scales

References: *Aviation Weather*, Chapter 2, "Atmospheric Energy and Temperature" and Appendix A, "Conversion Factors."

BACKGROUND DISCUSSION

The sun is the ultimate energy source for the atmosphere. Atmospheric motions are driven by temperature differences across the earth's surface. Those temperature differences are caused by variations in the amount of solar radiation absorbed at the earth's surface and by heat transfer throughout the atmosphere. The physical processes that link air motions to temperature differences will become clearer in later reading and exercises. In this exercise, you will do some simple tasks that will help you better understand how incoming solar radiation varies over the earth's surface due to latitude and to seasonal and daily changes in sun-earth geometry. You will briefly examine the concept of advection and learn some basic weather map interpretation techniques through the analysis of a mean temperature chart. Finally, a series of exercises are available to help you deal with the common use of both the Fahrenheit and Celsius temperature scales.

TASK 2-1: SUN-EARTH GEOMETRY.

The annual movement of the earth about the sun results in seasonal changes in the amount of solar radiation received at each latitude. For example, in the Northern Hemisphere winter, the sun's elevation angle is lower and the days are shorter than in the summer. These changes occur because of the 23.5° tilt of the earth's axis to the solar plane.

1. The solar plane is the two dimensional surface which passes through the center of the sun and the center of the earth. In fact, the entire orbit of the earth lies in the solar plane. In the following space, draw a diagram illustrating the solar plane. Show the location of the sun and the earth's orbit. Label the diagram clearly.

2. In figure 2-1, there are four diagrams of the earth and the sun (two solstices and two equinoxes). The observer's viewpoint is at the level of the solar plane. The parallel arrows on the right indicate the orientation of the incoming solar radiation. Show the orientation of the earth's axis to the solar plane in each diagram by drawing lines representing the axis of the earth and the equator (Be careful, in two of the diagrams, only one pole will be visible). Shade that portion of the earth that is untouched by the direct solar radiation in each diagram. In the spaces provided, identify the latitude where the sun's rays are perpendicular to the earth's surface.

NAME: _____

DATE: _____ CLASS: _____

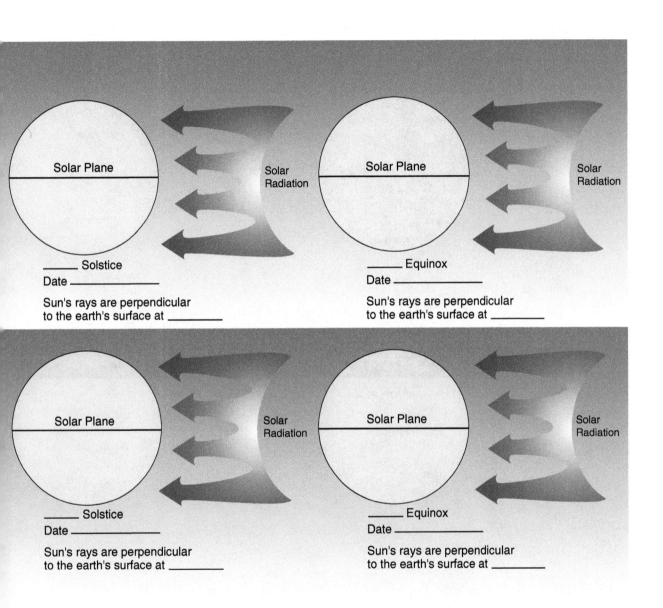

Figure 2-1. Orientation of the Earth to the Sun.

3. In figure 2-2, label the **elevation angle** of the sun.

Figure 2-2. Solar Elevation Angle.

NAME: _____

DATE: _____   CLASS: _____

4. The noontime solar elevation angle, e, for a station at latitude, L, is given by

$$e = 90 - (L-L_p)$$

where L is the latitude of the observer and L_p is the latitude where the sun's rays are perpendicular at noontime. In table 2-1, verify that e has been computed correctly for the first two cases and compute e for the last five cases.

TABLE 2-1

DETERMINATION OF NOONTIME ELEVATION ANGLE

Location	L (°)	Date	L_p (°)*	e (°)
North Pole	90N	September 23	_____	0
Denver	40N	June 22	_____	73.5
Mexico City	19.5N	December 22	_____	_____
South Pole	90S	December 22	_____	_____
Melbourne	38S	March 21	_____	_____
Miami	25.5N	June 22	_____	_____
London	51.5N	December 22	_____	_____

* L and L_p are positive angles in both hemispheres **except** when L is in the opposite hemisphere from L_p. In the latter case, L_p is negative.

TASK 2-2: DIURNAL VARIATION OF SOLAR RADIATION AND TEMPERATURE.

The temperature of the atmosphere is the result of the transfer of energy from the sun to the earth and the redistribution of energy within the atmosphere. Near the ground, atmospheric temperatures are ideally measured at a height of one meter in a ventilated shelter protected from the direct radiation of the sun. These temperatures are often called surface air temperatures or simply "surface temperatures."Be careful not to confuse these temperatures with ground temperatures, which are sometimes referred to as "surface temperatures," and temperatures measured at higher levels, which are called "upper air temperatures." The regular, daily increase and nightly decrease in surface air temperature is due to the daily cycle of incoming solar radiation caused by the rotation of the earth. Table 2-2 gives the hourly values of solar elevation angle for two widely separated locations.

TABLE 2-2

Hourly solar elevations (°) for Point Barrow, Alaska, and Tucson, Arizona, for the same day. Elevation angles are only shown for those hours when the sun is above the horizon. Times of sunrise and sunset are also indicated (e = 0). Hourly surface air temperatures are also listed for Tucson for the same day. The Tucson skies are clear. Only Local Standard Times (LST) are shown.

Location	Pt. Barrow, AK 71.3°N 156.78°W	Tucson, AZ 32.1°N 110.9°W	
Time (LST)	e (°)	(e°)	T (°F)
0600			52
0642		Sunrise	
0700		3.1	51
0800		14.5	56
0900		25.1	62
1000		34.0	67
1022	Sunrise		
1100	1.3	40.3	73
1200	3.1	42.9	77
1207		43.0 Solar Noon	
1300	3.9	41.3	81
1310	4.0 Solar Noon		
1400	3.5	35.8	84
1500	2.0	27.3	85
1557	Sunset		
1600		17.1	84
1700		5.7	82
1733		Sunset	
1800			78

NAME: _____

DATE: _____ CLASS: _____

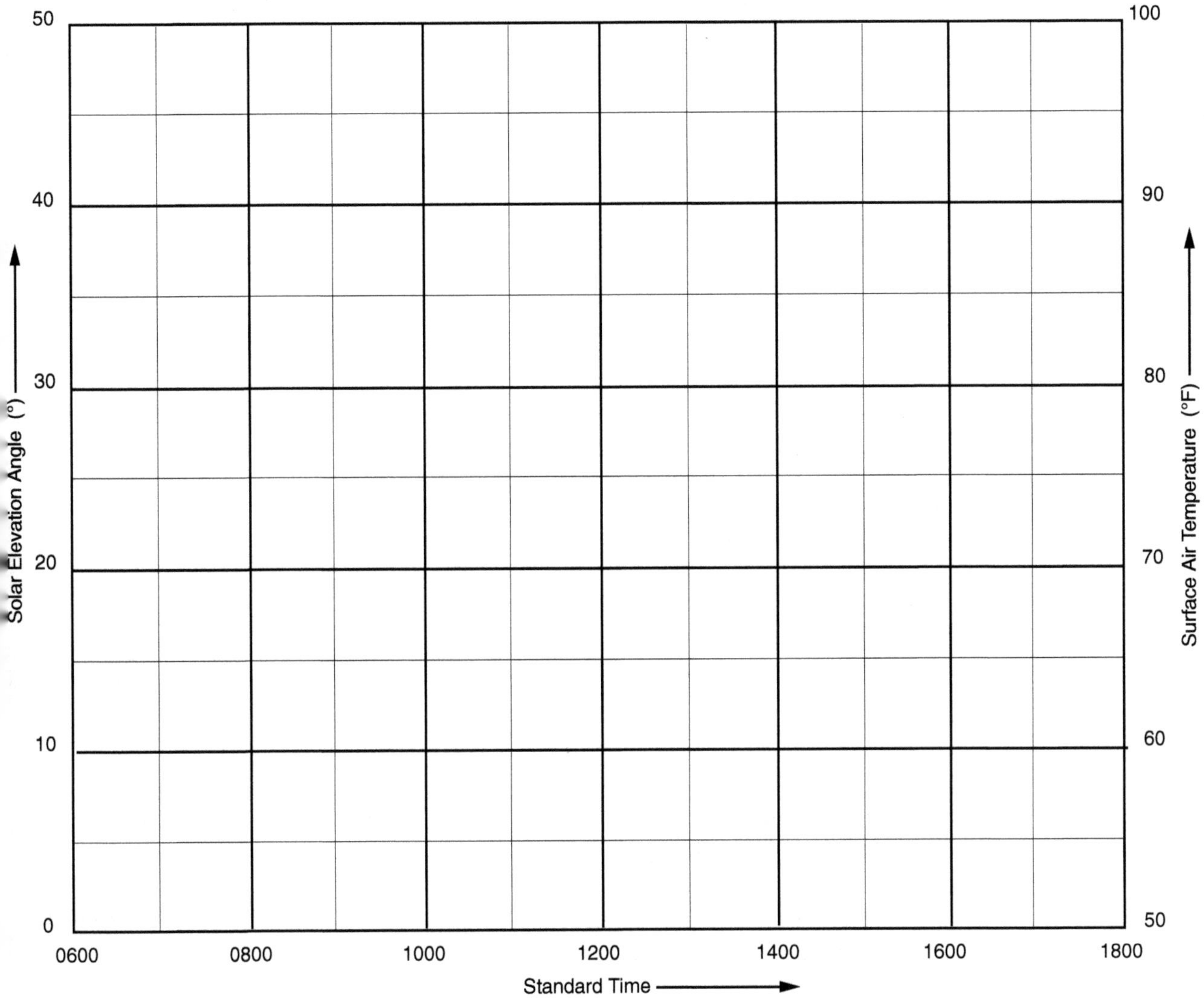

Figure 2-3. Plotting Chart for Tucson, AZ and Point Barrow, AK.

1. On figure 2-3, neatly plot elevation angles (y axis) versus hour (x axis) for both locations in table 2-2. Be sure to use the elevation angle scale on the left hand side of figure 2-3. Connect each series of points with separate, smooth curves. Label the curves clearly with the station names.

2. What season (or seasons) do these data represent? (Hint: consider the latitudes and the elevation angle at solar noon.)

3. If two stations are poleward of latitude 23.5°, the difference in noontime solar elevation angles is equal to their difference in latitude. Verify this for Tucson and Point Barrow.

4. Why does solar noon occur at 1207LST in Tucson and 1310LST at Point Barrow?

5. In a contrasting color, plot the Tucson hourly temperatures using the temperature scale on the right hand side of figure 2-3.

6. Why does the minimum temperature at Tucson occur at about sunrise and the maximum temperature occurs nearly three hours after solar noon?

CAUTION: If there are clouds present and/or strong temperature advection, temperature and radiation patterns can be significantly different than what is shown in figure 2-3. Some of these effects will be considered in later exercises.

NAME: _____

DATE: _____   CLASS: _____

TASK 2-3: CONVECTION AND ADVECTION.

In addition to the transfer of energy by radiation, heat energy can also be transferred by mass. The **vertical** transfer of heat by the transfer of mass is commonly referred to as convection. For example, when air is unstable, rising bubbles of relatively warm air (thermals) characterize the convective processes. Thermals tend to form over hot surfaces. Generally the hotter the surface, the stronger the thermals. The significance to aviation is that flight through thermals is turbulent. In later exercises, you will examine the subjects of atmospheric instability and turbulence in greater detail, but for the present task, this brief introduction is sufficient.

The **horizontal** transfer of heat by mass is called advection. For example, warm air moving from tropical regions into cooler northern latitudes is an example of "warm" advection. In future exercises, we will examine cases where distinct cold and warm advection occur in conjunction with cold and warm fronts, respectively. Meteorologists often use the term "advection" to generally indicate horizontal transfer of any substance by the transfer of mass. Therefore, we can speak of the "advection of moist air" or the "advection of polluted air."

Identify the following situations as "warm advection" or "cold advection."

1. Sea air moving inland during the afternoon (sea breeze). _____

2. Air moving from land to sea at night (land breeze). _____

3. Gusty outflow from a thunderstorm. _____

TASK 2-4: AVERAGE TEMPERATURE DATA.

If surface air temperatures are averaged over a long period of time, the day-to-night, and day-to-day fluctuations and random advective and convective changes would average out. A map of such averaged temperatures would reflect the strong influence of the distribution of solar radiation. Figure 2-4 is a map of values of average surface air temperatures for July plotted for several locations east of the Rocky Mountains.

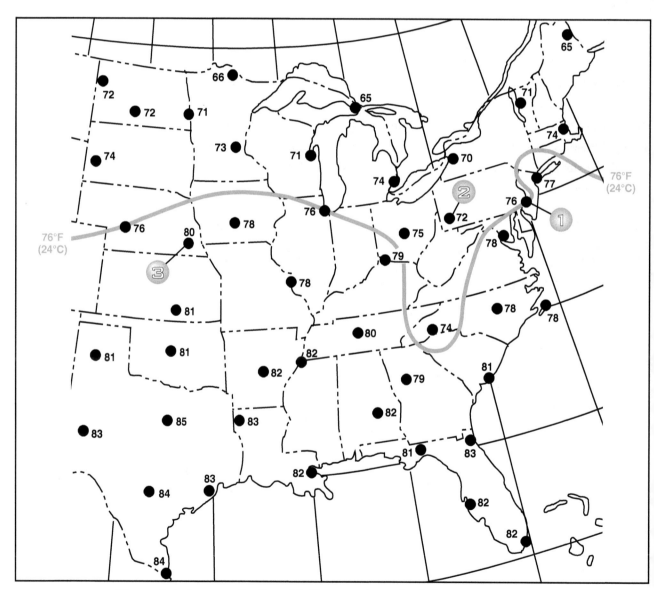

Figure 2-4. Average Surface Air Temperatures for July.

NAME: _____

DATE: _____ CLASS: _____

1. Analyze the temperature field in figure 2-4 by drawing lines of constant temperature (isotherms) at 3F° intervals across the map. The 76°F isotherm has already been drawn to help you get started.

   Use the following procedure to accomplish the analysis: Begin the analysis in an area where there is plenty of data. Draw isotherms between data points by interpolating the location of the isotherm by eye. As you analyze, remember that the lines you draw are continuous; that is, they must EITHER form closed curves OR end at the edges of the map. Lines of different values cannot touch each other. It helps to keep in mind that, as you draw each isotherm, it should divide the temperature field such that lower temperatures are always on one side of the isotherm and higher temperatures are on the other side. In addition to helping you understand the temperature climatology for the U.S., this "analysis" assignment will also prepare you to do analyses of other variables in later exercises (e.g. pressure).

2. At the edge of the map, label the ends of the isotherms in °F and °C.

3. Although areas 1, 2, and 3 in figure 2-4 are at about the same latitude and, therefore, receive approximately equal amounts of radiation at the top of the atmosphere, the average temperatures in those areas are different. In the space below, give a reasonable explanation why this temperature difference occurs.

4. Recall that the International Standard Atmosphere is an approximation of the real atmosphere and that actual temperature conditions may vary considerably from ISA values. The map that you analyzed in figure 2-4 shows average July temperatures. Since the ISA is representative of the entire year in midlatitudes, it should not be surprising that all the temperatures in figure 2-4 are warmer than standard. Confirm this by recording the coldest and warmest temperatures on the chart in table 2-3. Assume for the moment that the temperatures are sea level temperatures and compute the difference between those temperatures and ISA sea level temperature (15°C = 59°F).

TABLE 2-3
DEVIATIONS OF JULY AVERAGE SURFACE
TEMPERATURE FROM ISA

	Temperature T (°F)	Deviation $T - T_{ISA}$ (F°)
Lowest	_____	_____
Highest	_____	_____

---

5. In those locations where the surface temperatures are actually at some elevation above sea level, do you expect the actual surface temperature deviations from ISA to be larger or smaller than the values shown in table 2-3. Why? (Remember that you assumed that the temperature map was at sea level for the calculation in table 2-3.)

NAME: _____

DATE: _____ CLASS: _____

TASK 2-5: TEMPERATURE CONVERSIONS.

Many students find that having three separate temperature scales to deal with in meteorology is somewhat confusing. For example, in the U.S., public weather bulletins and forecasts are usually reported in degrees Fahrenheit. Aviation Routine Weather Reports (METARs) use degrees Celsius, while many meteorological computations require absolute temperatures (Kelvins). It is imperative that you know the differences between temperature scales. Here are a few simple exercises to help you get comfortable with °C and °F.

1. **Approximate Conversions Without a Calculator.** These are useful for quick "ballpark" estimates and to check yourself if you do an actual computation. Examine table 2-4. Notice that the table is easily reconstructed from memory if you keep just one set of numbers in mind (e.g., "room temperature"). All other sets are found by adding or subtracting differences of 18F° = 10C° from the original set (for example 68°F + 18F° = **86°F = 30°C** = 20°C +10C°). If you want to estimate intermediate temperatures, use increments of 9F° = 5C° or 1.8F° = 1.0C°.

TABLE 2-4
SOME SIMPLE CONVERSIONS

	°F		°C
A very hot day	104	=	40
A hot day	86	=	30
Room temperature	**68**	**=**	**20**
A cool day	50	=	10
Freezing (melting)	32	=	0
A very cold day	14	=	−10
Arctic Air	−4	=	−20

Do not refer to the list of numbers in table 2-4 and (without a calculator) give approximate conversions for the following temperatures. You want to be closer than 5F° and about 3C° in your estimates. The blank line to the far right will be used when you compute the exact conversion later in the task.

a. 25°C   = ___ °F ___

b. 41°F   = ___ °C ___

c. 77°F   = ___ °C ___

d. -10°C = ___ °F ___

e. 23°F   = ___ °C ___

f. 37°C   = ___ °F ___

g. 50°C   = ___ °F ___

h. -20°C = ___ °F ___

i. 40°C   = ___ °F ___

j. 5°F   = ___ °C ___

2. **Exact Conversions.** Exact conversions are accomplished by precise equations which are easily solved on a calculator. These equations depend on certain critical ratios. Complete the following:.

a. Boiling point of water   ____°F ____°C

b. Melting point of ice   ____°F ____°C

c. Difference   ____°F ____°C

d. You have just shown that an increment of ____ C° is equivalent to an increment of ____ F°. Note that the numbers that you just wrote down are INCREMENTS of temperature, not actual temperatures. Their ratios (reduced to their lowest common denominators) are

$$F°/C° = (fraction)\_\_\_\_ = (decimal) \_\_\_\_ \text{ and}$$

$$C°/F° = (fraction)\_\_\_\_ = (decimal) \_\_\_\_.$$

These are the key ratios used in the common sets of equations for converting temperatures from °F to °C and from °C to °F:

$$°C = 5/9(°F\text{-}32); °F = 9/5°C\text{+}32 \qquad \textbf{(1)}$$

or

$$°C = (°F\text{+}40)5/9 \text{ - } 40; °F = (°C\text{+}40)9/5 \text{ - } 40 \qquad \textbf{(2)}$$

Although both sets of equations return the same answers, **(2)** is easier to remember than **(1)**, because you simply add 40, multiply by the key ratio, then subtract 40.

NAME: _____

DATE: _____ CLASS: _____

e. Use either set of the equations written above to check the estimates that you made in task 2-5, question 1. Write the precise answers to the right of your estimates.

3. **More Temperature Conversion Exercises.** In table 2-5, convert the ISA temperatures to °F and Kelvin (K). Begin by making a mental estimate of the answers using the method introduced in task 2-5, question 1. Note that to the nearest whole degree, K = 273 + °C.

TABLE 2-5

	Altitude (feet MSL)	(°C)	Temperature (°F)	(K)
A.	5,000	5.1	_____	_____
B.	10,000	-4.8	_____	_____
C.	20,000	-24.6	_____	_____
D.	30,000	-44.4	_____	_____
E.	36,200	-56.5	_____	_____ (tropopause)

QUESTIONS

1. On the basis of geometry alone, explain why areas of the earth's surface in high latitudes receive less solar energy per hour during daylight than areas at low latitudes.

2. Most untrained observers who attempt to estimate elevation angles of the sun, other stars, or clouds do so erroneously. Design an experiment to test the validity of this statement.

3. When the sun is approximately vertical, a cloud at 15,000 feet AGL will cast a shadow on the ground that has the same horizontal dimensions as the cloud itself. Explain why this occurs.

4. Are there any times when the sun shines on the north side of a building located at a latitude north of 23.5°N? Explain.

5. Use an ordinary thermometer to measure the air temperature at heights of 2 inches, 4 inches, 20 inches, and 5 feet above the ground on a hot afternoon (be sure the sun doesn't shine directly on the thermometer) and on a clear, calm night. Plot your results on a piece of graph paper. Contrast and explain the results.

6. On a clear, calm morning, just before sunrise, measure the temperature of the air about an inch above the top surface of the wing of a small aircraft. Note the height of the point of measurement above the ground. Move away from the airplane and measure the air temperature at the same level in the open. Explain the results.

EXERCISE 3:

PRESSURE AND DENSITY ALTITUDE

OBJECTIVES:

- To understand how atmospheric pressure is measured, reported, and displayed
- To understand the interpretation and use of altimeter setting and related errors
- To understand the determination, interpretation, and use of density altitude

References: *Aviation Weather*, Chapter 3, "Pressure, Altitude, and Density"; Appendix A, "Conversion Factors"; Appendix B, "Standard Atmosphere"; and Appendix D, "Standard Meteorological Codes and Graphics for Aviation." Supplemental Reading: *AC 00-45F, Aviation Weather Services*, Section 4.

BACKGROUND DISCUSSION

Atmospheric pressure and its variations over space and time have important consequences for aviation. The distribution of pressure helps us identify weather systems. The difference in pressure over a horizontal distance is closely related to wind velocity. The difference in pressure over a vertical distance is the determining factor in defining altitude. Every pilot must understand atmospheric pressure, its measurement, and its aviation applications. In the following tasks, you will examine the procedure for determining station pressure, sea level pressure, and altimeter setting. You will familiarize yourself with the construction and use of surface pressure analyses and upper air constant pressure charts. You will learn to recognize important weather-producing features in the pressure field such as lows, highs, troughs, and ridges. You will investigate errors in pressure altimeter readings due to non-standard atmospheric conditions. Finally, the concept of density altitude will be examined and you will practice decoding atmospheric pressure information from the international METAR code.

TASK 3-1: STATION PRESSURE, SEA LEVEL PRESSURE, AND ALTIMETER SETTING.

In order to understand the differences among these three useful parameters, it is useful to examine the procedure used to determine their values.

1. **Raw Pressure Observation (P_r).** Raw pressure is what is measured at a particular location by a pressure instrument (e.g., mercurial barometer, aneroid barometer, pressure transducer). Some examples are given in table 3-1 for mercurial barometers located near 37°N. Convert all of the readings to mb (hPa) and round to the nearest tenth. If you have access to a mercurial barometer, add a reading for your location.

<table>
<tr><td colspan="2" align="center">TABLE 3-1</td></tr>
<tr><td align="center">P_r
(in. Hg.)</td><td align="center">P_r
(mb)</td></tr>
<tr><td align="center">30.000</td><td align="center">_____</td></tr>
<tr><td align="center">29.600</td><td align="center">_____</td></tr>
<tr><td align="center">30.020</td><td align="center">_____</td></tr>
<tr><td align="center">_____</td><td align="center">_____</td></tr>
</table>

2. **Instrument and Latitude (gravity) Corrections (C).** The raw pressure observation may require corrections due to instrument errors introduced in manufacturing and non-standard temperature conditions. When instruments are manufactured, they are calibrated to a set of standard conditions. Any deviation from these standards will require a correction to the measurement. The temperature error, for example, arises because the mercury in a mercurial barometer expands and contracts with temperature changes in the same manner as a mercurial thermometer. Ordinarily, the mercurial barometer is installed in a location where temperature changes are minimized. However, even slight changes are important and so mercurial barometers usually have an attached thermometer to monitor temperature changes.

Another correction to the raw observation is for latitude or gravity. Because the earth is not a sphere; the distance between an object on the surface and the center of the earth varies with latitude. Therefore, gravity also varies with latitude. In order to compare atmospheric pressure readings at different latitudes, all readings must be corrected to the standard latitude (45°). When the instrument and latitude corrections are applied to the raw pressure reading, the result is the Station Pressure (P_{sta}).

NAME: _____

DATE: _____ CLASS: _____

Table 3-2 lists the raw pressure readings from table 3-1, the thermometer readings **(T)**, and the corrections **(C)** for instrument, latitude, and temperature. Correct the raw pressures for the given C. Be sure you add the corrections algebraically. In this, and all subsequent calculations, compute pressures to .001 in. Hg. If you have access to a barometer and the appropriate corrections, compute the station pressure for your location.

TABLE 3-2

P_r (in. Hg.)	T (°F)	C (in. Hg.)	P_{sta} (in. Hg.)
30.000	70	−0.135	_____
29.600	60	−0.106	_____
30.020	58	−0.100	_____
_____ *	___	_____	_____

* If your measurement of P_r is in mb (hPa), be sure your correction is in the same units to find P_{sta}.

---

3. **Altitude Correction.**

Since all observation stations are not at the same altitude and because the change of pressure with height is much greater than any change of pressure over a similar horizontal distance, each observation must be "reduced" to a common altitude (sea level). In this way, small but important, horizontal pressure differences between stations can be accurately determined. This altitude correction is determined by estimating the temperature conditions for a hypothetical atmospheric layer between the station altitude and sea level. Sea Level Pressure (P_{slp}) is then extrapolated from the station pressure on the basis of hydrostatic balance. The accepted technical procedure for computing P_{slp} includes the use of a time-averaged station temperature and an involved equation with adjustments for errors that occur in mountainous areas. In order to demonstrate the impact of the altitude correction, we will use a simplified procedure that will give approximate results.

In table 3-3, transfer the station pressures (P_{sta}) that you computed in table 3-2. Station altitudes (Z) above sea level are given. Estimate the altitude correction (C_z) for each reading by noting that in the lower atmosphere pressure decreases **approximately*** one inch of mercury for every thousand feet of altitude (0.1 inch per 100 feet). Indicate whether the correction is added to (+) or subtracted from (-) the station pressure to find P_{slp}. Finally, compute the sea level pressures and convert your answers to mb (hPa). Spaces are provided for your own local measurements.

P_r (in. Hg.)	P_{sta} (in. Hg.)	Z (ft)	C_z (in. Hg.)	P_{slp} (in. Hg.)	P_{slp} (mb)
30.000	_____	300	_____	_____	_____
29.600	_____	1000	_____	_____	_____
30.020	_____	0	_____	_____	_____
_____	_____	_____	_____	_____	_____

TABLE 3-3

* **Although pressure ALWAYS decreases with height, it decreases more rapidly with height in cold air and less rapidly with height in warm air.**

4. **Altimeter Setting.** There are several ways to determine the altimeter setting. When your aircraft is on the ground, set the altimeter to the field elevation, then read the altimeter setting from the barometric scale window on the altimeter. The altimeter setting also can be computed by extrapolating sea level pressure from station pressure by assuming that the hypothetical atmosphere between station elevation and sea level is the standard atmosphere. This is done by applying a correction factor for the difference between actual field elevation and field elevation in the standard atmosphere. This procedure is different than the procedure described earlier for the computation of P_{slp}. In the latter case, NON-STANDARD temperature conditions are taken into consideration. This means that a simple conversion of sea level pressure from millibars to inches of Mercury will NOT necessarily give you the altimeter setting, unless the station is at sea level. The pressure altimeter presumes standard conditions.

NAME: _____

DATE: _____ CLASS: _____

Consider the following: if the field is located at sea level and the pressure is 30.42 inches (one-half inch greater than standard), then the field elevation in the standard atmosphere is about 500 feet above sea level. Another way of saying this is that if you were flying your airplane at an altitude of 500 feet above sea level with the altimeter set at 29.92, your altimeter would read 0 feet. By adjusting the altimeter to 30.42 inches it would read 500 feet.

In the space below, draw a cross section illustrating the above example. Your cross section should show the aircraft path at its true altitude (a solid line), and two dashed lines, one showing the location of the 29.92 in. Hg. pressure level and the other showing the 30.42 in. Hg. pressure level. Clearly label each line.

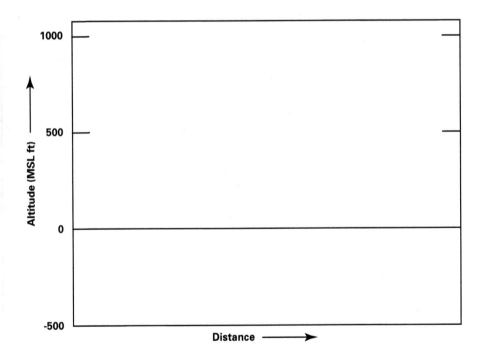

TASK 3-2: PRESSURE FIELD ANALYSIS.

Figure 3-1 is a simplified surface analysis chart. For the purposes of this task, only the observed sea level pressure (SLP) data are plotted for the time and date of the chart. The SLP data are plotted in whole millibars.

1. Analyze the pressure field in figure 3-1. Begin by visually examining the data field, noting where the highest and lowest pressures are located. Next, draw lines of constant pressure (isobars) every four millibars. Use 1000 mb as the starting point and draw isobars at 992, 996, 1000, 1004, 1008 mb, etc. Label each isobar with its pressure value. Keep in mind that the pressure values are valid at the location indicated by the dot. The 1012 mb isobar (labeled 12) has been drawn on the chart to get you started. The same analysis rules that you used for isotherms in Exercise 2, Task 2-4, Question 1 also apply here. Review them before you start to draw the isobaric patterns.

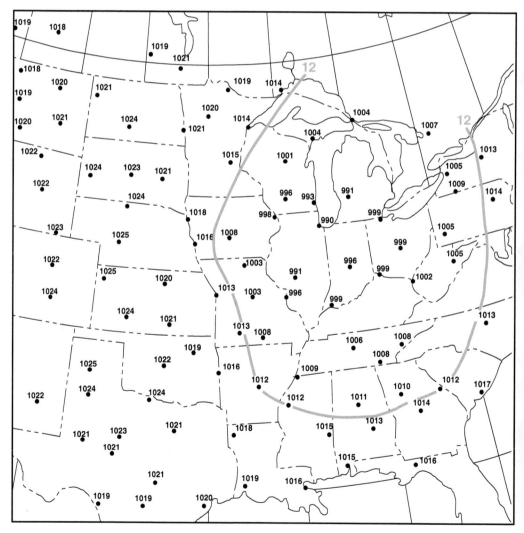

Figure 3-1. Simplified Sea Level Pressure Chart.

NAME: _____

DATE: _____ CLASS: _____

2. After the chart has been analyzed, it is standard procedure to identify the locations of the centers of high and low pressure areas. A pressure center is a point in the pressure field that has a relatively larger or a relatively smaller value of pressure than the surrounding area. A pressure center is analogous to a mountain peak or the lowest point in a nearly circular valley on a topographical chart. On your analysis of figure 3-1, mark each pressure center with a small circled "x." From the analysis, interpolate an estimate of the pressure at that center point. Print that value immediately north of the pressure center. At each center of relatively high pressure, write a blue block "H" for high. Similarly, use a red block "L" for low in each center of relatively low pressure. Examples of these labels are shown below.

3. In addition to the pressure centers, pressure gradients are important because of their relationship to the wind. This relationship will be examined in later exercises. For the present, it is important that you become familiar with the definition and patterns of pressure gradients. A pressure gradient is the difference in pressure divided by the distance over which the difference is measured. A pressure gradient is always measured perpendicular to the isobars. When the pressure gradient is "strong," isobars are packed closely together. If the pressure gradient is "weak," the isobars are spread out. In figure 3-1, circle the region of strongest pressure gradient on the chart and label it "strong."

TASK 3-3: SURFACE ANALYSIS CHART.

Consider the Surface Analysis Chart in figure 3-2. This chart was selected for this exercise because it combines a large amount of plotted METAR data in conjunction with the analysis. Most surface analysis charts available for briefing show far less (if any) data. However, plotted METAR reports are often available on separate charts which are easier to read. Your main goal in this particular task is to develop an understanding of the link between pressure observations and the sea level pressure analysis.

1. Raw data are plotted for each reporting station on the map. The pressure analysis is similar to what you did in the previous task, but for different data. Because of the need to display pressure data and several other pieces of information in the small area around each station location, those data are coded. However, decoding is easy because the data always appear in the same location relative to the position of the station and the codes are simple. A simplified plotting model is shown below for temperature, pressure, and three-hour pressure change **(pressure tendency)**.

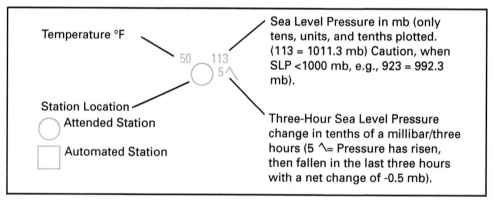

In table 3-4, list the surface air temperatures, sea level pressures, and pressure tendencies at the numbered stations on figure 3-2. Make sure to include the units of measure for each item.

TABLE 3-4

	Temperature	Station Pressure	Pressure Tendency
1	_____	_____	_____
2	_____	_____	_____
3	_____	_____	_____

NAME: _____

DATE: _____ CLASS: _____

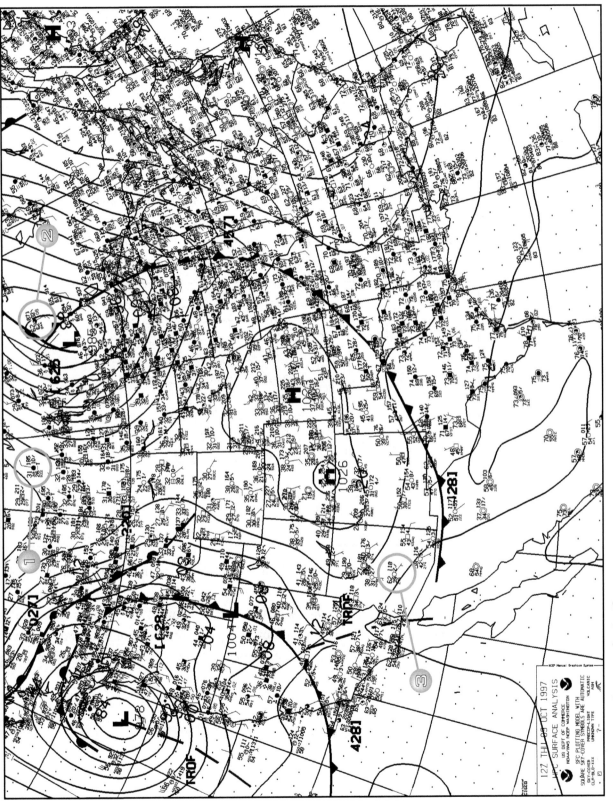

Figure 3-2. Surface Analysis Chart.

2. To make sure that you understand the sea level pressure pattern, carefully trace a red line over the entire lengths of the 1020 mb and 996 mb isobars in figure 3-2. Note the differences in labeling of the centers of the pressure areas.

3. In figure 3-2, circle regions of strongest sea level pressure gradient and the weakest sea level pressure gradient. Label them "strong" and "weak," respectively.

4. A ridge in the pressure field is an elongated region of relatively high pressure. A ridge line is the axis of the ridge. If it is located properly, pressure will always **decrease** as you move perpendicularly away from the ridge line. Locate a distinct ridge of high pressure in figure 3-2. Use the following examples to draw a ridge line (heavy, "wiggly" line) along the ridge axis and label it "ridge."

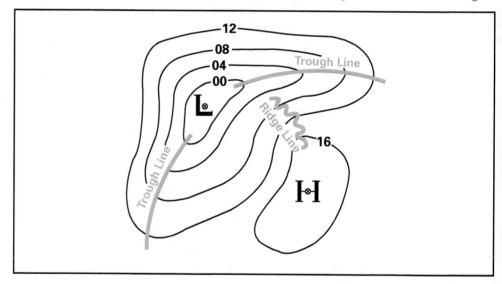

5. A trough in the pressure field is an elongated region of relatively low pressure. A trough line is the axis of the trough. If it is located properly, pressure will always **increase** as you move perpendicularly away from the trough line. Locate a distinct trough of low pressure in figure 3-2, draw a heavy solid line along its axis, and label it "trough" (sometimes abbreviated "TROF").

NAME: _____

DATE: _____ CLASS: _____

TASK 3-4: CONSTANT PRESSURE CHART.

While a surface chart has isobars to delineate the pattern of sea level pressure, the upper air charts that are used by meteorologists are constant pressure charts, which show spatial variations of the height of that pressure surface. In order to show the height variations, contours (lines of constant height) are drawn instead of isobars. The reason for this convention is that certain calculations are greatly simplified for the meteorologist. For the aviator who uses these charts for flight planning, contour patterns can be interpreted in the same manner as isobaric patterns with regard to the location of centers of lows and highs, troughs, ridges, and the evaluation of gradients. Although the difference between the actual height and the standard height of a constant pressure surface is important for wind velocity determinations, that difference is typically a small fraction of the total pressure height. Therefore, for descriptive purposes, a constant pressure chart can be viewed as nearly flat and near its standard height. See table 3-5.

TABLE 3-5		
STANDARD HEIGHTS OF CONSTANT PRESSURE CHARTS		
Pressure	**ISA Pressure Altitude**	
Millibars	**Feet**	**Meters**
850	4,781	1,457
700	9,882	3,012
500	18,289	5,574
300	30,065	9,164
250	33,999	10,363
200	38,662	11,784

1. A series of constant pressure charts is given in figure 3-3. The pressure levels are indicated on each chart. Fill in the data in the box on each chart, including the standard height to the nearest 1,000 feet.

2. As with the surface analysis, raw upper air data are plotted for each reporting station on the map. A simplified plotting model is shown below for temperature and height of the pressure surface.

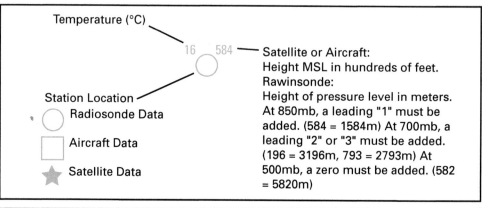

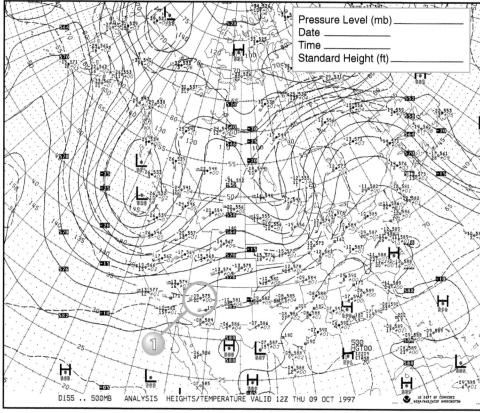

Figure 3-3. Constant Pressure Charts.

NAME: _____

DATE: _____ CLASS: _____

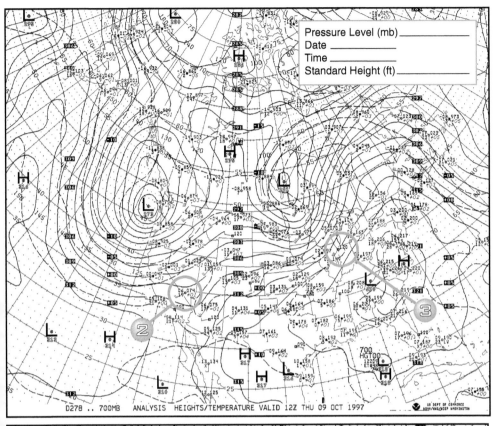

Pressure Level (mb) _____
Date _____
Time _____
Standard Height (ft) _____

D278 .. 700MB   ANALYSIS HEIGHTS/TEMPERATURE VALID 12Z THU 09 OCT 1997

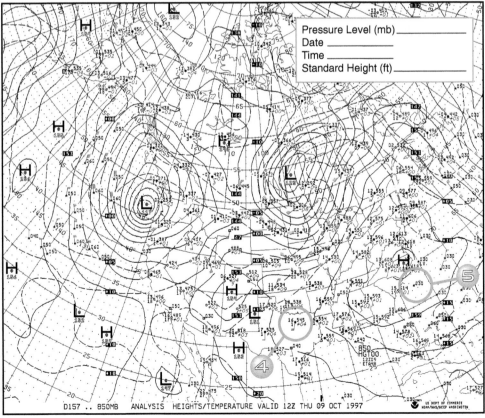

Pressure Level (mb) _____
Date _____
Time _____
Standard Height (ft) _____

D157 .. 850MB   ANALYSIS HEIGHTS/TEMPERATURE VALID 12Z THU 09 OCT 1997

For the numbered stations in figure 3-3, list the altitude of each report in table 3-6. Also list the temperature (if available) and the observation type (radiosonde, aircraft, satellite).

TABLE 3-6

	Altitude (MSL)	Temperature (°C)	Observation Type
①	_____	_____	_____
②	_____	_____	_____
③	_____	_____	_____
④	_____	_____	_____
⑤	_____	_____	_____

3. Using the same techniques as in tasks 3-3, locate and label, in black, one prominent trough line, one prominent ridge line, and the area of the strongest contour gradient on each of the constant pressure charts in figure 3-3. Keep in mind that the contours on those charts are the solid lines. Also note that, on all constant pressure charts, the contours are labeled in tens of meters.

4. The dashed lines on each of the constant pressure charts are isotherms at 5C° intervals. In red, trace over the following isotherms at the designated pressure levels: +10°C at 850 mb, 0°C at 700 mb, and -20°C at 500 mb. Notice that in the mid-troposphere (500 mb), highs and ridges tend to be warmer than their surroundings and lows and troughs tend to be colder.

5. Interpolate temperature values from the isotherm pattern at 45°N 135°W on each chart and place the answers in table 3-7.

TABLE 3-7

850 mb _____ °C

700 mb _____ °C

500 mb _____ °C

NAME: _____

DATE: _____ CLASS: _____

TASK 3-5: PRESSURE ALTIMETER ERRORS.

A triangular flight track is shown on the sea level analysis of figure 3-4. You fly from A to B to C and then back to A. Assume that the altimeter setting is given by the sea level pressure shown on the map and, initially, the temperature conditions are standard for the entire route of flight.

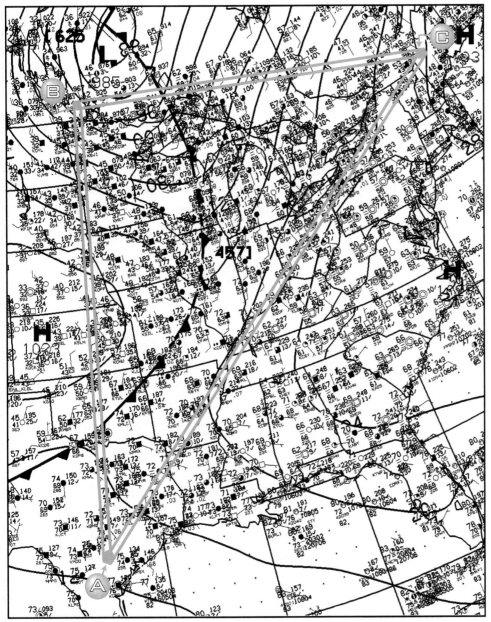

Figure 3-4. Portion of a Surface Analysis Chart

1. You set your altimeter at point A just prior to takeoff. Thereafter, you only reset your altimeter at the endpoint of each leg (in reality, this is a bad pro-

cedure). In table 3-8 enter the sign (+, -, 0) of the altimeter error at each end-point; that is, before you reset your altimeter for the next leg. Note: Error = True Altitude - Indicated Altitude. If the error is positive, you are high. If the error is negative, you are low.

TABLE 3-8	
Endpoint	Altitude Error (+, −, 0)
B	_____
C	_____
A	_____

2. The change in the altitude reading on the altimeter is approximately 10 feet for a change of 0.01 in. Hg. in altimeter setting. What would the approximate altitude error be including the sign before resetting your altimeter at point B. Show your work below. Hint: you will have to do some conversions from millibars to inches here.

3. Now consider the pressure altimeter error that would arise because the atmospheric temperature is non-standard. Assume that the surface temperature in figure 3-4 is representative of the air layer between your aircraft and the ground (that is, if the surface air temperature is below standard, then the whole layer is below standard). At each point (A, B, and C) will an altimeter that has the proper setting still have an error due to non-standard temperature? If so, what will be the sign of the error? If the error is positive, you are high. If the error is negative, you are low. Enter the sign of the temperature error in table 3-9.

TABLE 3-9	
Endpoint	Temperature Error (+, −, 0)
B	_____
C	_____
A	_____

NAME: _____

DATE: _____ CLASS: _____

TASK 3-6: METAR.

Surface weather observations are communicated in international METAR code. With this exercise, you begin a formal study of METAR code that will continue in the succeeding exercises. Knowledge of the code will provide you with access to valuable weather information. Weather codes by themselves can be uninteresting topics; however, METAR is more than a code. It is an extremely useful learning tool. It will teach you to "speak the language" of meteorology so that you can understand the procedures by which weather is observed. The code will provide you with a checklist of critical weather parameters that must be examined in every complete preflight. These benefits will provide impetus for you to learn the code and to practice reading it at every opportunity.

A list of coded METAR observations follows. Your task is to decode a portion of the reports using the code breakdown provided in Appendix D of *Aviation Weather*, and then to write the decoded information in table 3-10, providing units where appropriate.

```
KAPA 160145Z 22005KT 30SM BKN100 BKN200 21/11 A2999=
KASE 160145Z 15005KT 7SM VCSH FEW030 OVC120 12/10 A3019=
KBJC 160150Z 23012G18KT 40SM SCT080 BKN160 23/09 A2998=
KBKF 160155Z 20008KT 25SM SCT060CB BKN120 BKN250 20/10 A2996 RMK SLP081 VIRGA
 ALQDS CB ALQDS MOV NE=
KCAG 160153Z AUTO 31006KT 10SM CLR 17/07 A3001 RMK A02 SLP111 T01720067 TSNO=
```

TABLE 3-10
DECODED METAR DATA

Station Identifier	Date	Time (UTC)	Temperature (°C)	Altimeter (in. Hg.)	Remarks (Pertinent to Pressure)
KAPA	_____	_____	_____	_____	_____
KASE	_____	_____	_____	_____	_____
KBJC	_____	_____	_____	_____	_____
KBKF	_____	_____	_____	_____	_____
KCAG	_____	_____	_____	_____	_____

TASK 3-7: DENSITY.

From earlier exercises and previous tasks in this exercise, you are aware of the vertical distribution of pressure and temperature in the standard atmosphere. For example, by now, you should know the appropriate altitude of the 500 mb pressure level and the temperature at the tropopause level in the standard atmosphere. With this task, you begin to familiarize yourself with the variation of density with altitude in the standard atmosphere. In the next task, you will examine the impact of non-standard density. Table 3-11, taken from Appendix B in *Aviation Weather*, shows the ratio between the air density at a given altitude and the sea level density for the ISA. This density ratio makes it easy to see the rapid decrease in density at low altitudes and the slower decrease aloft.

TABLE 3-11
ISA DENSITY RATIO

Altitude (ft MSL)	Density Ratio*
0	1.00
1,000	0.97
2,000	0.94
3,000	0.92
4,000	0.88
5,000	0.86
6,000	0.84
8,000	0.79
10,000	0.74
15,000	0.63
20,000	0.53
30,000	0.37
40,000	0.24
50,000	0.15
60,000	0.09

*rounded

1. Under standard sea level conditions, the pressure, temperature, and density ratio are

    P _____ T _____ Density Ratio _____

NAME: _____

DATE: _____ CLASS: _____

2. At what altitudes does the density in the ISA decrease to the following fractions of its sea level value? (Interpolate altitudes from table 3-11.)

0.75 _____ feet MSL

0.50 _____ feet MSL

0.25 _____ feet MSL

0.10 _____ feet MSL

TASK 3-8: DENSITY ALTITUDE.

As you may know, low atmospheric density conditions can cause an aircraft to perform poorly. This is particularly critical during takeoff and climb. Therefore, it is useful from the points of view of both performance and safety to keep track of density conditions. The concept of "density altitude" is an important factor in determining aircraft performance. Density altitude is the altitude (MSL) where the density in the standard atmosphere is equal to the actual density. Put another way, density altitude is simply the pressure altitude corrected for non-standard temperature. The lower the actual density is below standard, the higher the density altitude is above actual field elevation.

1. Consider a hot summer day where the pressure at sea level is the same as standard, but the temperature is 86°F (30°C). As you would expect from the gas law, under these conditions, the sea level density is lower than standard. Verify this statement by writing the gas law (Chapter 1, *Aviation Weather*) to show that if pressure is constant, as temperature increases, density decreases.

2. For the situation described in question 1, the actual elevation of the airport is sea level. Use figure 3-6 to determine the density altitude for the temperature and pressure conditions given in 1. An example is given explaining how the figure is used. Do the example before you attempt the problem.

Density Altitude _____

3. (optional) If you have a flight computer, check your answer in 2.

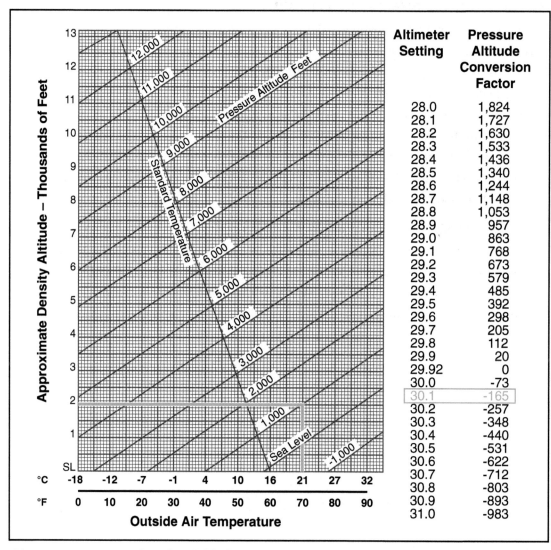

Figure 3-6. Density Altitude. Field elevation is 1,165 feet, non-standard pressure correction is –165 feet, pressure altitude is 1,000 feet, and temperature is 70°F (21°C). Enter the table at the temperature, move vertically to the pressure altitude line, and then move horizontally to the left to read the density altitude, 2,000 feet.

NAME: _____

DATE: _____ CLASS: _____

QUESTIONS

1. A series of METAR reports is given below. Decode date, time, temperature, and all related pressure information including altimeter setting.

```
KPRC 160145Z VRB05KT 65SM SCT050 BKN150 20/17 A3013=
KSDL 160147Z 30010KT 35SM SCT100 BKN250 34/16 A2989=
KSOW 152350Z 22005KT 40SM FEW015 OVC060CB 17/15 A3020 RMK TS OCNL LTGICCG OHD
 VCSH SW SH DSNT NE TCU DSNT E NOSPECI 70051 T01670150 402330156=
KTUS 160156Z 26007KT 10SM FEW060CB 28/21 A3000 RMK AO2 SLP114 CB DSNT W MOV NE
 T02782711=
KYUM 160156Z 26007KT 10SM SCT050CB SCT120 BKN200 32/22 A2981 RMK SHRAE33 CB SW
 MOV NE SLP091 P0000 T03170222
```

2. Why do meteorologists find the analysis of the sea level pressure field so useful?

3. Why is sea level pressure rather than station pressure analyzed on sea level pressure charts?

4A. Use your flight computer or figure 3-6 to compute density altitude for the following conditions:

Temperature	Field Elevation (ft MSL)	Altimeter Setting (in. Hg.)	Density Altitude (ft)
80°F	5,000	29.80	_____
75°F	3,500	30.60	_____
4°C	2,000	30.00	_____

4B. (Optional) You are departing an airport where the airport pressure altitude is 5,000 feet and the temperature is 40°C. How will your rate of climb and take-off distance be affected? With your instructor's guidance, locate a "Koch Chart" to estimate your answer.

5. Explain "High to low, look out below!"

6. If you set your altimeter to 29.92 inches of mercury and you fly at an indicated altitude of 14,000 feet, what is the pressure at that level to the nearest whole millibar?

EXERCISE 4:

WIND

OBJECTIVES:
- To familiarize you with atmospheric winds including characteristics and causes, technical nomenclature, reporting procedures, mapping, and applications
- To increase your ability to interpret wind information for flight planning purposes

References: *Aviation Weather*, Chapter 4, "Wind" and Appendix D, "Standard Meteorological Codes and Graphics." Supplemental Reading: *AC 00-45F, Aviation Weather Services*, Section 4.

BACKGROUND DISCUSSION

The term wind velocity, or simply wind describes the horizontal movement of air. It plays an extremely important role in aviation. Wind can impact navigation by increasing or decreasing groundspeed or causing the aircraft to drift from its intended track. It can create a variety of hazards ranging from windshear to clear air turbulence. Therefore, your knowledge of the causes and characteristics of the wind is invaluable in the your study of aviation.

Wind is a direct result of a horizontal difference in pressure between two points. Other forces, including Coriolis force and frictional force, arise when the air is in motion. The observation and description of wind velocity is different than pressure and temperature. Pressure and temperature each require only **one** measurement, whereas wind velocity is a **vector**, which requires **two** measurements, windspeed and wind direction. Furthermore, wind reporting requires added information about wind shifts, gusts, and peak wind. This exercise helps you better understand and interpret basic wind information by examining the relation of wind to pressure on both surface and upper air charts. You will learn to read conventional wind reports by decoding and encoding data. The usefulness of wind data also will be demonstrated with a simple flight duration problem.

TASK 4-1: METAR.

One of the first and most important elements in METAR code is wind direction and speed. The wind to which these terms refer is often called the "sustained wind."

1. Define "sustained wind."

2. Define "gust" as it is used in METAR code.

3. Define "peak wind" as it is used in METAR code.

NAME: _____

DATE: _____ CLASS: _____

4. Decode all wind information in the following METAR reports and place the information in table 4-1:

```
KAEX 242150Z 30010KT 7SM OVC035 27/23 A2980=

KLCH 242151Z VRB03KT 3SM -RA BR FEW077 OVC015 25/24 A2978 RMK AO2 SLP092 P0063
  T02500244=

KPOE 242155Z 31009G16KT 6SM BR SCT020 BKN025 BKN050 BKN070 27/22 A2979 RMK
  SLP085 8/570 9/520=

KDLH 242155Z 27019G31KT 10SM CLR 21/09 A2971 RMK AO2 PK WND 27034/2144 SLP062
  T02110089=

KEVM 242155Z AUTO 26014KT 7SM CLR 23/07 A2966 RMK A01=

KINL 242155Z AUTO 26015G19KT 10SM CLR 25/09 A2959 RMK AO2 PK WND 27026/2135 SLP020
  TO2500094=
```

TABLE 4-1
DECODED WIND DATA

Station	Sustained Wind Direction (°)	Speed (Kts)	Gust Speed (Kts)	Peak Wind Direction(°)	Speed (Kts)	Time of Occurrence (UTC)
KAEX	_____	_____	_____	_____	_____	_____
KLCH	_____	_____	_____	_____	_____	_____
KPOE	_____	_____	_____	_____	_____	_____
KDLH	_____	_____	_____	_____	_____	_____
KEVM	_____	_____	_____	_____	_____	_____
KINL	_____	_____	_____	_____	_____	_____

5. Figure 4-1 is a time record of wind speed and direction. Create a METAR for-matted wind report from the 1100 PST data. Encode time (UTC), sustained windspeed and direction, gusts, and peak wind data. Place the coded data in the space at the top of the next page.

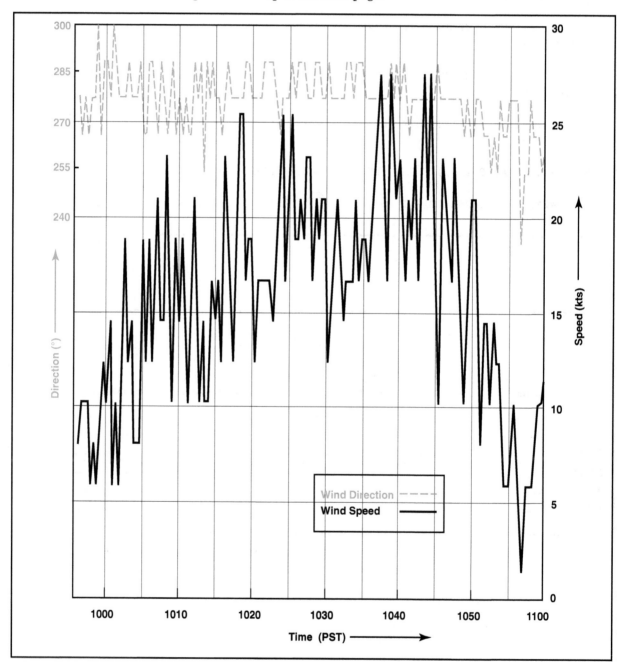

Figure 4-1. Plot of Wind Speed and Direction. This figure represents a one-hour record of the wind. Time is located along the x-axis, the solid line and right-hand y-axis represent speed, and direction is shown by the blue dashed line and left-hand y-axis.

NAME: _____

DATE: _____ CLASS: _____

TASK 4-2: WINDS AND WEATHER MAPS.

Wind information is critical for flight planning. Much of that information is available in graphical format on weather maps. In this task, you will learn to interpret wind information directly from plotted data and indirectly from isobars and contours. Also, you will examine the effects of friction on the wind.

1. As shown in the top part of figure 4-2, wind direction information is often shown on weather maps with "wind arrows" which fly with the wind; that is, toward the station model circle. All directions are relative to true north. By convention, these arrows have no arrowheads, but do have tail feathers. Wind speeds to the nearest five knots are indicated with feathers at the rear and on one side of the arrow. These are best interpreted as "sustained winds." Gusts are not always shown. When they are plotted, the letter "G" appears at the end of the wind barb, followed by the observed gust speed. In the lower part of the figure are wind plots numbered one through six. North is at the top of the page. Write the wind direction in degrees and the wind speed in knots below each wind plot.

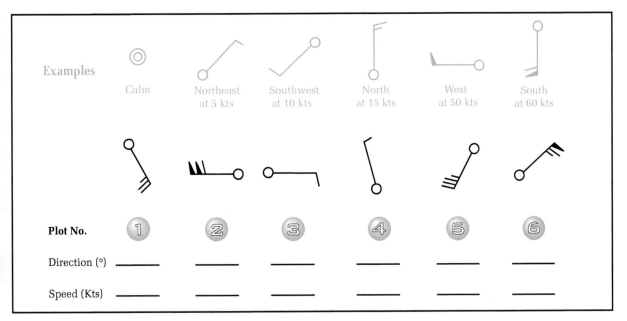

Figure 4-2. Wind Plotting Conventions.

2. Figure 4-3 shows a 500 mb constant pressure chart. Note: north-south is not necessarily toward the top of the chart, but is parallel to longitude lines. Similarly, east-west is parallel to latitude lines. Always determine the plotted wind direction relative to the "local" orientation of the chart coordinate system. At observation points one and two, what are the wind directions and speeds for the circled stations?

   ① Direction _____° Speed _____ kts

   ② Direction _____° Speed _____ kts

3. Use symbols similar to those in figure 4-2 to plot a wind with a direction of 230° and a speed of 35 knots at 45°N and 140°W on figure 4-3.

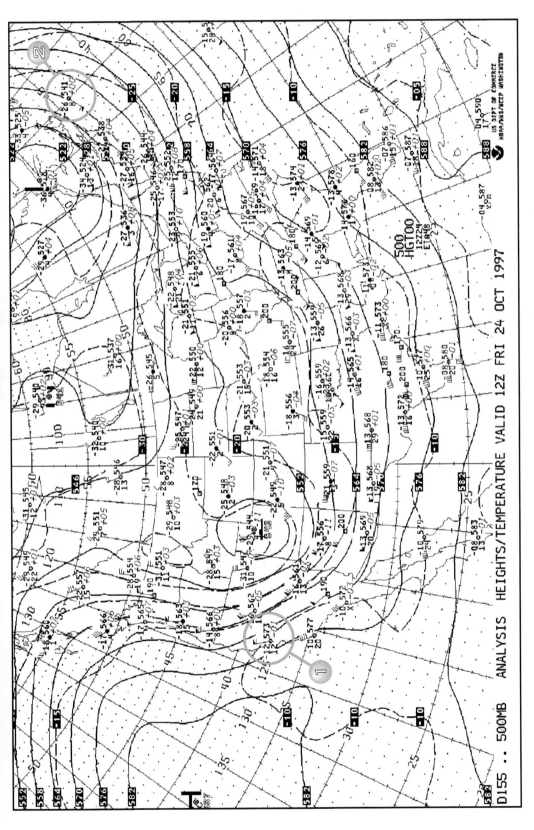

Figure 4-3. 500 mb Constant Pressure Chart.

TASK 4-3: GEOSTROPHIC WIND.

When the atmosphere is moving in response to horizontal pressure gradients that extend over hundreds of miles or more, the motion is usually close to geostrophic balance. This is a fortunate situation because it allows you to deduce wind speeds and directions from pressure patterns alone.

1. Define "geostrophic wind." Draw a diagram of the geostrophic wind. Be sure to include the pattern of isobars, the balance of forces, and the geostrophic wind vector. Label clearly.

2. Evidence of approximate geostrophic balance can be seen in upper air charts, especially away from the friction at the surface. Figure 4-4 is a 500 mb chart and is well away from the earth's surface, except in areas of very high mountains. In the spaces provided below, write the geostrophic wind direction for points one through four. Remember, if the winds are in geostrophic balance, the lower values of 500 mb heights will be on the left looking downwind in the Northern Hemisphere.

   ① Direction _____ °

   ② Direction _____ °

   ③ Direction _____ °

   ④ Direction _____ °

3. Inspect the contour gradient for locations one through four in figure 4-4. Which location has the strongest geostrophic wind? _____

NAME: _____

DATE: _____ CLASS: _____

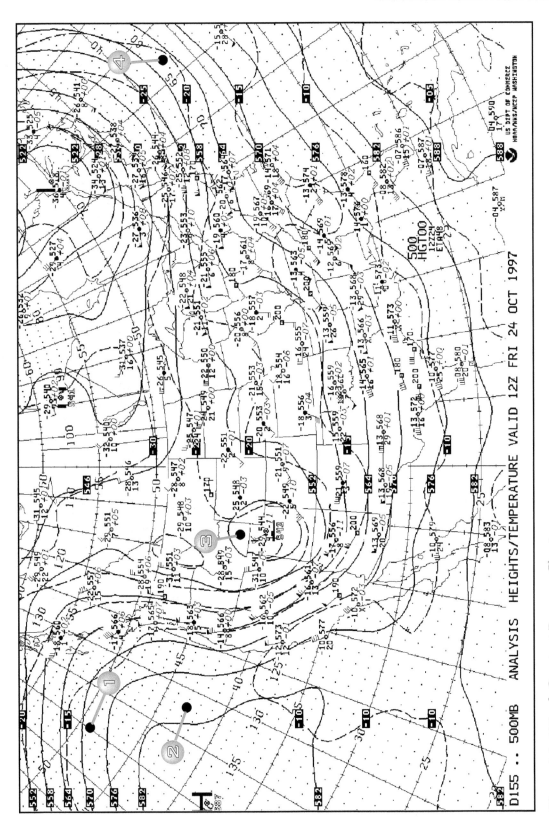

Figure 4-4. 500 mb Constant Pressure Chart.

TASK 4-4: FRICTIONAL FORCE.

Figure 4-5 is a surface analysis chart. At this level, frictional force does not allow, a geostrophic balance between pressure gradient force and Coriolis force. Evidence of this can be seen in the difference between the actual and the geostrophic wind directions.

1. At points one through six in figure 4-5, determine the geostrophic wind direction according to the orientation of the isobars and the actual wind direction from the reported values. Enter your answers in spaces below.

	A Geostrophic Direction (°)	B Reported Direction (°)	C A − B (°)
①	_____	_____	_____
②	_____	_____	_____
③	_____	_____	_____
④	_____	_____	_____
⑤	_____	_____	_____
⑥	_____	_____	_____

2. Compute the individual differences between the geostrophic and actual wind directions in question 1 (geostrophic direction minus actual direction). Be sure you indicate the sign (±) of the difference. Then, compute the average difference. Average _____ °

3. Would you expect the difference to be more or less over water? Why?

NAME: _____

DATE: _____ CLASS: _____

4. Wind directions often change significantly in the first few thousand feet above the ground. This change is important in takeoff and landing operations. What would be a good estimate of wind directions at 2,000 feet AGL for points one through six in figure 4-5?

1 ____ °

2 ____ °

3 ____ °

4 ____ °

5 ____ °

6 ____ °

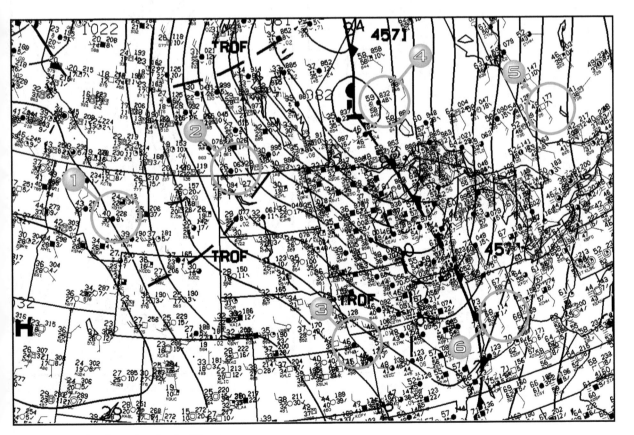

Figure 4-5. Surface Analysis Chart.

5. Which point in figure 4-5 has the strongest pressure gradient? _____ At that point, draw a prominent arrow on the chart that indicates the direction of the pressure gradient force.

TASK 4-5: WINDS ALOFT AND FLIGHT PLANNING.

You are considering a flight along track A-B shown on the two charts in figure 4-6. You intend to fly out (A-B) at about 10,000 feet MSL and back (B-A) at about 18,000 feet MSL. Your actual airspeed is 200 kts at both altitudes. Use the information from figure 4-6 to estimate the total duration of your flight. For this problem, ignore the time necessary to climb and descend. Show your work clearly in the space below figure 4-6. (Hint: you will have to measure the length of the track and estimate the average windspeed along the track at each level.) Remember, one degree of latitude is approximately 60 nautical miles. If you have a flight computer, do the problem by hand first and then check it with your flight computer.

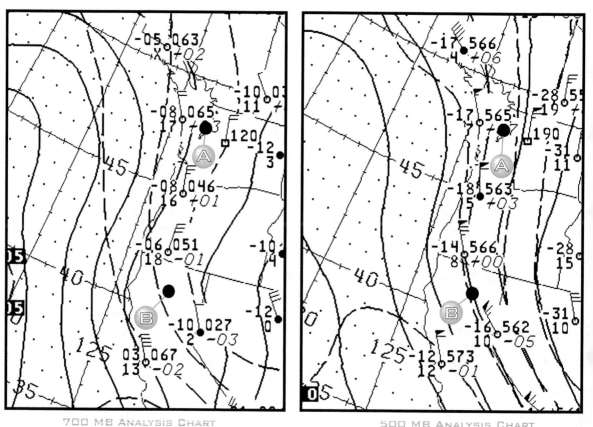

Figure 4-6.

NAME: _____

DATE: _____ CLASS: _____

QUESTIONS

1. Near the surface of the earth in the Northern Hemisphere, winds around low pressure areas blow (clockwise/counterclockwise) _____ and (inward/outward) _____. Winds around high pressure areas tend to blow _____ and _____.

2. Answer question 1 for the Southern Hemisphere.

3. Explain how friction interferes with geostrophic balance.

4. Draw a diagram that shows a balance of forces on a horizontally moving air parcel when pressure gradient, Coriolis, and frictional forces are the only forces present. Show isobars, wind vector, and force vectors. Be sure that the forces balance. Label the diagram clearly.

5. For very small scales, Coriolis force is too small to have much of an effect on the horizontal movement of air parcels (the wind); therefore, geostrophic balance (can/cannot) _____ exist and the wind usually blows from (high/low) _____ pressure toward (high/low) _____ pressure.

6. With your instructor's guidance, select an "out and return" flight plan similar to Task 4-5, but for a different time and location. After you specify your route, use the Aviation Weather Center web site http://aviationweather.gov/. Click on "Standard Briefing" and select appropriate winds aloft information to estimate your approximate flight duration.

EXERCISE 5:

STABILITY AND VERTICAL MOTION

OBJECTIVES:
- To help you better understand the concept and evaluation of atmospheric stability
- To familiarize you with processes which produce vertical motions

Reference: *Aviation Weather*, Chapter 5, "Vertical Motion and Stability"

BACKGROUND DISCUSSION

Atmospheric motion is more frequently noticeable in the horizontal direction where winds vary from light breezes to jet stream winds of well over 100 knots. With a few notable exceptions, such as thunderstorms, the vertical movement of the atmosphere is much less dramatic, but even its small movements have an immense importance in the creation of weather. Away from the earth's surface, the majority of clouds are produced by upward-moving moist air and dissipated by downward-moving air. Therefore, vertical movements of air are critical to the presence or absence of IFR conditions. Also, aircraft encounters with the stronger up- and downdrafts are felt as turbulence. A thorough understanding of the processes that cause vertical motions is critical for safe flight. A list of some of these processes, and typical and extreme vertical motions are shown in figure 5-1, in *Aviation Weather*.

In addition to understanding the causes of vertical motion, it is very important to grasp the concept of atmospheric stability (and instability). For example, it is more difficult, but not impossible, for a stable atmosphere to produce substantial vertical motions. On the other hand, it is very easy for an unstable atmosphere to produce vertical motions that are often strong. If there is sufficient water vapor, upward motions in a stable atmosphere produce broad, smooth layers of stratiform clouds, while upward motions in an unstable atmosphere produce turbulent cumuliform clouds, such as those associated with thunderstorms. Therefore, the processes that produce vertical motions in the atmosphere must be considered together with stability concepts.

In the present exercise, you will complete tasks designed to familiarize you with stability concepts. In order to keep these new ideas manageable, we will only consider stability for the dry atmosphere. Later exercises will apply these concepts to the cloudy (moist) atmosphere. Also, you will do some simple computations to demonstrate some mechanisms that cause vertical motions.

TASK 5-1: STABILITY AND AIR PARCELS.

Atmospheric stability is a basic concept that is important for understanding causes of many aviation-critical weather phenomena. These include thunderstorms, windshear, turbulence, fog, low ceilings, and freezing rain, to name a few. This portion of this exercise, in conjunction with the associated reading in the text, provides the essential background for understanding stability.

As you move through the task, it is important to learn and apply the proper terminology. For example, the term stability is used to describe the general topic. When we analyze the "stability" of the atmosphere, we describe it in specific terms, such as stable, unstable, or neutral. Thus, when we discuss the "instability" of the atmosphere, we are referring to the degree to which the atmosphere is unstable. On the other hand, reference to "stability" must be taken in context; it means either a reference to the degree to which the atmosphere is stable or to the general topic.

A stable atmosphere resists vertical movements. In a stable environment, air can still move up and down, but with difficulty. Also, to rise or sink, stable air needs a continuous supply of "outside help," such as a mountain, a front, or convergence or divergence of airflow. Stable air produces smooth cloud layers such as stratus.

When air is unstable, it moves upward and/or downward simply because it is positively or negatively buoyant. It needs no "outside help" after its initial push upward or downward. Unstable air can "overturn" easily and, sometimes, violently. Unstable air produces clouds with vertical development such as cumulus. In this task, you will learn to evaluate stability on the basis of the relative temperature and behavior of displaced air parcels.

1. An air parcel is said to be **stable** if, when displaced upward, its temperature is (warmer than, colder than, equal to)_____ the temperature of its surroundings.

2. An air parcel is said to be **neutral** if, when displaced upward, its temperature is (warmer than, colder than, equal to)_____ the temperature of its surroundings.

3. An air parcel is said to be **unstable** if, when displaced upward, its temperature is (warmer than, colder than, equal to)_____ the temperature of its surroundings.

4. In the questions above, precisely define the phrase "the temperature of its surroundings."

5. The rate at which dry air cools as it rises is _____ C°/1,000 feet, which is known as the _____ lapse rate.

6. In table 5-1, you are given some air temperature observations (T_a) that were obtained at the indicated levels during a climb to 5,000 feet. You want to know if air rising from the surface will be stable, unstable, or neutral. You will see in later exercises that this type of calculation is useful for evaluating potential thermal lift for gliders and the likelihood of thunderstorms.

Inspect the data in table 5-1 and "lift" an air parcel from the surface to each succeeding level and determine its temperature at each level (T_p). Place your answers in column A. Keep in mind that the air is dry and that it cools due to expansion as you lift the parcel. Also note that temperature data are not all at 1,000-foot intervals.

TABLE 5-1

Altitude ft AGL	Air T_a °C	A Parcel T_p °C	B Difference $[T_p-T_a]C°$	C Direction of Acceleration (Upward/Downward)
0	12	12	0	_____
1,000	7	_____	_____	_____
2,000	4	_____	_____	_____
3,500	2	_____	_____	_____
4,000	2	_____	_____	_____
5,000	4	_____	_____	_____

NAME: _____

DATE: _____ CLASS: _____

7. Determine whether the "lifted" parcel temperature is colder or warmer than the surrounding air temperature at each level by subtracting the air temperature from the parcel temperature [T_p-T_a]. If the parcel temperature is warmer than the air temperature, the difference is positive (+). If the parcel temperature is colder, the difference is negative (-). Place your answers, including the sign, in column B.

8. After a parcel is displaced upward, if it is **warmer** than the surrounding air, it is **unstable**. It will **accelerate** upward, away from its initial level. Upward speed will increase as the parcel rises. If an air parcel is displaced upward and it is **colder** than its surroundings, it is **stable**. It will accelerate downward, back toward its original level.

   It is important to clearly understand the difference between "speed" and "acceleration." For example, if an air parcel is moving upward and it becomes colder than its surroundings **it will be accelerated downward, but it can still be moving upward**; that is, its upward speed will slow. A good analogy of this process can be found with a pendulum when it swings upward. Because it is being accelerated downward by the gravitational force as it moves upward, it slows down. As with the air parcel, the pendulum will finally stop its upswing and move in the opposite direction.

   In table 5-1, inspect column B for each level and indicate in column C those levels where the air parcel will be **accelerated** upward or downward.

9. In the space below, explain what happens when a downward moving cold parcel moves into a layer where it is suddenly warmer than its surroundings.

10. It is often useful to determine atmospheric stability layer by layer. The question you are asking is "If a parcel of air at the bottom of a certain layer (not necessarily at the surface) is displaced to the top of the layer, will it be stable, unstable, or neutral?" Answer this question using the data in table 5-2. The measured air temperatures at the top of each layer have been carried forward from table 5-1. Displace a parcel from the bottom to the top of each layer to determine the temperature difference between the displaced parcel and its surroundings. Complete sections A, B, and C. To help you get started, the computations have been done for the first two layers.

TABLE 5-2

Layer ft AGL	Air T_a°C	A Parcel T_p°C	B Difference $[T_p-T_a]$C°	C Layer Stability: Stable (S), Unstable (U), Neutral (N)		
Ground level	12	12	0			
0 – 1,000	7	9	2	S	<u>U</u>	N
1,000 – 2,000	4	4	0	S	U	<u>N</u>
2,000 – 3,500	2	———	———	S	U	N
3,500 – 4,000	2	———	———	S	U	N
4,000 – 5,000	4	———	———	S	U	N

TASK 5-2: STABILITY AND SOUNDINGS.

The parcel method is useful for visualizing the stability evaluation process, but it is awkward to apply. An easier way to evaluate stability is by comparing lapse rates from actual temperature soundings with the adiabatic lapse rate. This method is easily seen with a plotted sounding. Figure 5-1 is a graphical presentation of the altitude and temperature data from table 5-1. Notice that altitude is displayed along the vertical axis and temperature along the horizontal axis. The heavy blue line represents the actual air temperature. Recall that the points along this line were **measured**. This line is often referred to as the "sounding" or "the sounding curve." The sounding lapse rate (LR) is defined as,

$$LR = \frac{(T_{lower} - T_{upper})}{(Z_{upper} - Z_{lower})}$$

where T_{lower} is the temperature measured at altitude, Z_{lower}, at the bottom of the layer and T_{upper} is the temperature measured at altitude Z_{upper}, at the top of the layer. If the temperature **decreases** with an **increase** in altitude, **LR > 0;** and if the temperature **increases** with an **increase** in altitude, **LR < 0** and an **inversion** layer exists. If the temperature is **constant** with an **increase** in altitude, **LR = 0** and an **isothermal** layer exists.

The parallel dashed lines sloping from lower right to upper left in figure 5-1 are **dry adiabats**. Their slopes correspond with the dry adiabatic lapse rate (DALR). You gave a numerical value for DALR in task 5-1, question 5. The dry adiabats indicate how a parcel of air will cool with upward movement and will warm with downward movement. If you want to know how any parcel will cool

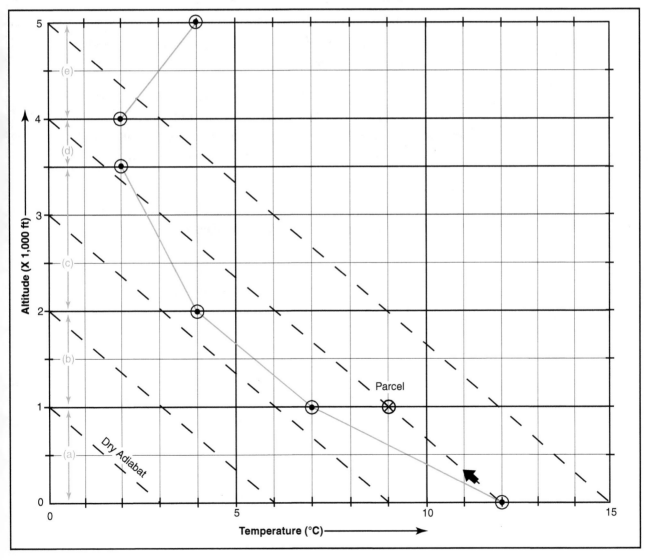

Figure 5-1. Sounding Diagram.

adiabatically, first locate the parcel on the diagram according to its initial temperature and altitude. Then, move parallel to the nearest dry adiabat to the final altitude and read the parcel temperature from the horizontal scale.

To practice using lapse rates and soundings to determine stability, you will redo the two stability evaluations you did task 5-1. Recall that you evaluated the stability of a parcel lifted from the surface, then you evaluated the stability of parcels in individual atmospheric layers.

1. **Parcel Stability.** A parcel with an initial temperature of 12°C, when lifted from the ground will follow the "path" (dashed line) indicated by the bold arrow in figure 5-1. At 1,000 feet AGL, the parcel will have a temperature of 9°C. The temperature of this parcel was computed in table 5-1. Notice in figure 5-1 that the parcel lifted to 1,000 feet will be clearly warmer than its surroundings and it is, therefore, unstable. If you continue to move the parcel along the same dry adiabat, all of the answers in table 5-1 are easily found.

   Shade in red the area between the sounding and the dry adiabat where the parcel lifted from the surface is warmer than its surroundings and in light blue to show where the parcel is colder than its surroundings. Compare the results with column B in table 5-1. They should be identical.

2. **Layer Stability.** The sounding in figure 5-1 is divided into layers as indicated by the blue letters in parentheses on the left-hand side of the diagram. In this exercise, you will evaluate the stability of each layer.

   a. Begin by establishing stability criteria. In figure 5-2, draw three straight lines that are examples of soundings for stable, unstable, and neutral layers. Label them clearly.

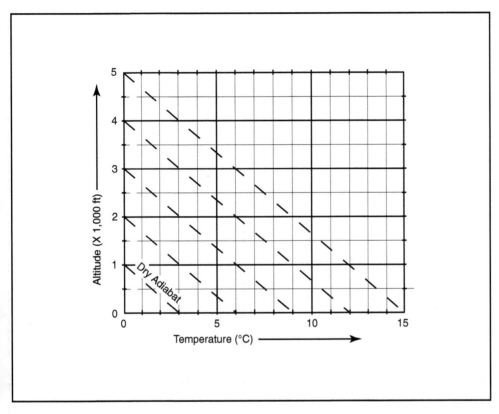

Figure 5-2. Sounding Diagram.

b. Now, using the soundings you constructed in figure 5-2 for reference, compare the lapse rates in each of the layers of figure 5-1 with DALR to determine its stability. Label each layer on the right hand side of the diagram with "S" (stable), "U"(unstable), or "N"(neutral). Compare the results with column C in table 5-2. The results should be identical. If they are not, recheck both of your solutions.

c. In red, neatly identify and label any layers in figure 5-1 that have isothermal lapse rates or inversions.

d. A more complicated sounding is shown in figure 5-3. Evaluate the stability of the indicated layers and label each layer with "S", "U", or "N" on the right hand side of the sounding. Also identify and label (in red) any isothermal or inversion layers.

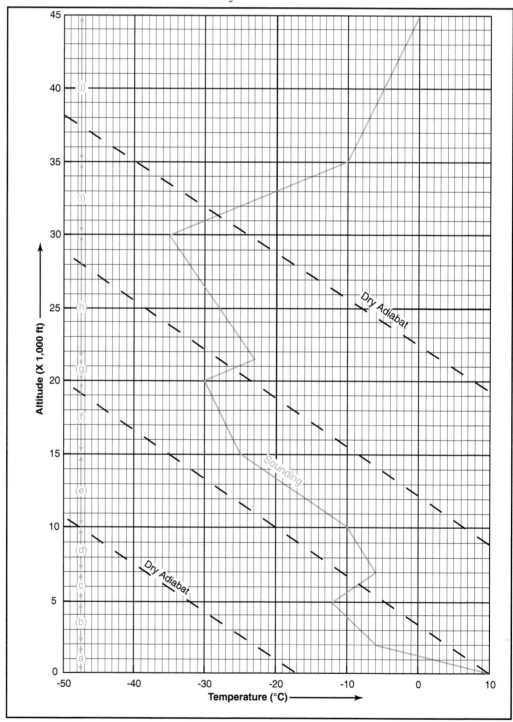

Figure 5-3. Sounding.

NAME: _____

DATE: _____   CLASS: _____

TASK 5-3: VERTICAL MOTIONS CAUSED BY HILLS AND MOUNTAINS.

Figure 5-4 shows a cross sectional view of an idealized ridgeline. The wind is blowing directly across the ridge from left to right. The air is forced up the windward side of the mountain and down the leeward or downwind side. Although this is a simplified picture of what goes on around real mountains, it will help you understand the importance of the mountain slope and the wind speed in producing strong up- and downward motions near mountains.

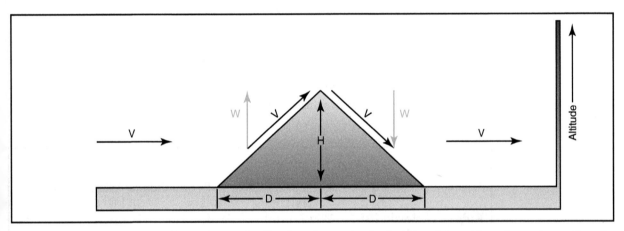

Figure 5-4. Cross Section Through an Idealized Ridge. H is the height of the ridge above the valley; D is one-half the width of the ridge. V is the horizontal wind speed perpendicular to the ridgeline and W is the upward or downward motion generated when the horizontal wind intersects the slope.

When air blows against a slope, it is deflected upward. Another way of saying this is that part of the horizontal motion becomes vertical motion. It turns out that the ratio of the vertical speed (W) to the horizontal speed blowing directly toward the ridge line (V) is exactly equal to the ratio of the height (H) to half of the width of our simple ridge (D); that is,

$$\frac{W}{V} = \frac{H}{D}. \qquad (1)$$

H/D is also known as the slope of the ridge (rise over run). The vertical motions produced by the wind are positive on the upwind side and negative on the downwind side. From **(1)**, if we know V and H, the W is simply

$$W = \frac{V \times H}{D}. \qquad (2)$$

This simple equation should agree with your experience: under similar wind conditions, wide, short mountains produce weaker up- and downdrafts than narrow, tall mountains.

Consider an example: if the ridge is 2,000 feet tall and 1 nautical mile wide (D = 3,040 feet) and the wind perpendicular to the ridgeline is 20 knots, then from equation **(2)**, the vertical motion is approximately

$$W = \frac{20 \text{ knots} \times 2,000 \text{ feet}}{3,040 \text{ feet}} = 13.16 \text{ knots} = 1334 \text{ fpm}$$

This calculation shows that, under the given conditions, there is air moving upward at 1,334 fpm on the upwind side of the ridge and downward at 1,334 fpm on the downwind side. This example corresponds with a very steep ridge. Up- and downdrafts of this magnitude would be reported as "moderate turbulence."

1. Table 5-3 shows heights and the widths for three ridges. Complete the table for the wind conditions given. Note the ridge "height" is height above the nearby valley or surrounding plains, not necessarily MSL. Also note that, in all cases, the wind direction is 90° to the ridgeline.

TABLE 5-3

Ridge	Height (ft)	Half Width (nm)	Perpendicular Wind Speeds 10 kts W (fpm)	30 kts W (fpm)	50 kts W (fpm)
a.	900	10	_____	_____	_____
b.	5,000	200	_____	_____	_____
c.	7,000	15	_____	_____	_____
d.	_____	_____	_____	_____	_____
e.	_____	_____	_____	_____	_____

2. In table 5-3, extra spaces are given for you to make computations for prominent hills or mountain slopes in your local area or for some other area where you fly.

CAUTION: Conditions can be more complicated and very dangerous due to the added effects of convection, mechanical turbulence, mountain lee waves, and the presence of clouds in the vicinity of mountains.

NAME: _____

DATE: _____ CLASS: _____

TASK 5-4: VERTICAL MOTIONS AND FRONTS.

Fronts are covered in great detail in later exercises. For the moment, we simply want to know how they create vertical motions. Fronts are common phenomena outside the tropics. By definition, a front is a boundary between dense air (usually cold) and less dense air (usually warm). The fronts you see on weather maps are often hundreds of miles long. A simple model of a front is a cold wedge of air lifting warm air ahead of it. Figure 5-5 shows both perspective and cross sectional views of a front.

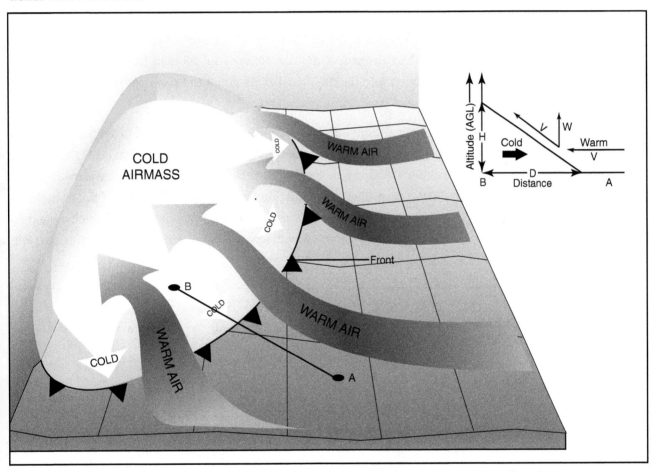

Figure 5-5. Three-dimensional perspective view (left) and cross sectional view (right) of a front. The location of the cross section (A-B) is shown in the perspective diagram.

A front is not a substantial surface like a mountain; however, air tends to move over frontal surfaces rather than through them. In this case, vertical motions along a front arise quite like they do over the slope of a mountain. Similarly, the magnitude of the vertical motion is proportional to the wind speed perpendicular to the front on the warm side and to the slope of the front. Whether the vertical motion is up or down (+ or -), depends on whether the wind relative to the front is directed toward or away from the front. In figure 5-5, it is directed toward the front. Fronts that produce clouds and weather are typically associated with warm, moist air rising over a wedge of cold air.

Given the relative speed of the warm air moving toward the front (V), the vertical motion (W) can be estimated as

$$W = V \times S.$$

In this case, S is the slope of the front; that is, the height of the frontal surface AGL divided by the perpendicular distance to the cold front (H/D in the cross section in figure 5-5). Notice that H/D is equal to "rise over run" as in the preceding task.

1. Some typical frontal slopes are given in table 5-4 together with wind speeds perpendicular to (toward) the front in the warm air. Assume that these fronts are either stationary, or moving so slowly that they can be considered stationary. Determine the vertical motions and the altitude (AGL) of the frontal surface 100 nm into the cold air for each of the following cases. Sketch a diagram of each situation. Label each diagram clearly with distances, altitudes, and wind speeds.

TABLE 5-4			
Frontal Slope	**Wind Speed (kts)**	**W (fpm)**	**Altitude of Front (ft AGL)**
1/400	5	_____	_____
1/100	15	_____	_____
1/250	15	_____	_____

NAME: _____

DATE: _____ CLASS: _____

CAUTION: The vertical motions computed here are estimates of those caused by fronts alone. They do not reflect the influence of embedded thunderstorms or underlying terrain.

CAUTION: Computations made here were for stationary fronts. Fronts often move with speeds of 10 to 40 knots. In these cases, the wind speed (V) relative to the front is the reported wind speed moving toward the front PLUS the speed of the front. For example, if the wind blowing toward the front has a speed of 15 kts and the front is moving in the opposite direction at 30 kts, V would be 15 + 30 = 45 kts and the upward motions generated by the front would be three times the stationary case.

QUESTIONS

1. This exercise has only touched on some of the causes of vertical motions in the atmosphere. Write a complete list of all causes of vertical motions.

2. Redo the 30-knot cases in table 5-3 for a situation where the wind is at an angle of 60° to the ridgeline (rather than 90°). Draw a diagram showing how you made your computations.

3. Compare the results of your vertical motion calculations in tables 5-3 and 5-4. What do you conclude about the impact on aircraft of the vertical motions caused by topography versus those produced by fronts? (Compare magnitudes and be sure that you review **cautions**.)

NAME: _____

DATE: _____ CLASS: _____

4. Following an early morning launch in a flight-for-distance competition involving gas (closed) balloons, competitors were trying to reach an altitude with favorable winds. One balloon could not get through an inversion until its occupants dumped some ballast. Why was the inversion a problem?

5. Generally, unstable conditions are associated with good visibilities (away from clouds) while stable conditions are associated with poorer visibilities. Why?

6. Which is more stable? An isothermal or an inversion layer? Why?

7. Occasionally, very fast-moving fronts are found on the leading edge of cold air. These fronts have much steeper slopes than those listed in table 5-4, especially within one or two thousand feet of the ground. Compute the magnitude of the vertical motion for such a front with a slope of 1/10 moving southward at 40 knots into a south wind of 20 knots. Show all of your work. Be sure to review **cautions**.

EXERCISE 6:

ATMOSPHERIC MOISTURE

OBJECTIVES:
- To familiarize you with measurements and calculations of moisture variables
- To understand coded reports and graphic presentations of moisture information

References: *Aviation Weather*, Chapter 6, "Atmospheric Moisture"; Appendix A, "Conversion Factors"; Appendix D "Standard Meteorological Codes and Graphics for Aviation"; Appendix C "Dewpoint and Humidity Tables"; and Appendix E "Glossary of Weather Terms." Supplemental reading: *AC 00-45F, Aviation Weather Services*, Section 2.

BACKGROUND DISCUSSION

Water vapor, water, and ice are essential ingredients of weather and aviation weather hazards. A thorough understanding of these subjects will enhance your own safety, as well as the safety of your passengers. In this exercise, you will examine the measurements and calculations of some of the most common moisture variables. These include wet bulb temperature, dewpoint, vapor pressure, saturation vapor pressure, relative humidity, and temperature-dewpoint spread. You will also decode METAR reports with emphasis on temperature and dewpoint. Finally, you will interpret temperature and dewpoint information displayed on surface analysis and constant pressure charts.

TASK 6-1: MOISTURE DEFINITIONS AND MEASUREMENTS.

Water vapor in the atmosphere is not directly measured. Rather, a number of other more easily measured variables are used to calculate the amount of water vapor. The instruments used to measure these variables will vary, depending on who is making the measurement, such as a state or federal agency, private citizen, or foreign government. Where possible, electronic measurements are the preferred mode because of their speed, accuracy, and dependability. In this exercise, the basic measurements were derived from a psychrometer because of its simplicity and because it gives you a clear physical interpretation of the physics of the measurement. Regardless of the types of instruments used, if they are similar in accuracy, precision, and calibration, the results will be identical. Figure 6-1 shows two examples of psychrometers.

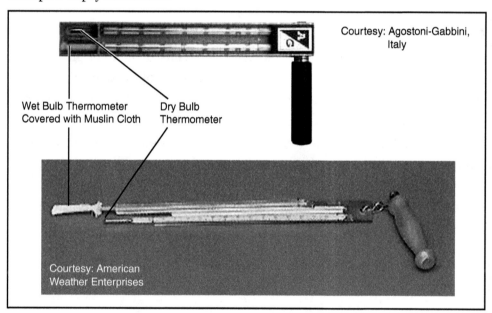

Figure 6-1. Basic Psychrometer Construction.

A psychrometer is a combination of two separate thermometers. The ones shown in figure 6-1 are liquid-in glass (for example, a mercurial thermometer). When used properly, the psychrometer will give you a measurement of the air temperature (also called the **Dry Bulb** temperature, **T**) and the **Wet Bulb** temperature **(WB)**. The end of the WB thermometer is encased in a muslin wick that is saturated with distilled water just before a measurement. The psychrometer is then ventilated by an electric fan or manually swung in a circle (a "sling" psychrometer). The psychrometers in figure 6-1 have handles for this purpose.

NAME: _____

DATE: _____ CLASS: _____

The wet bulb temperature is the lowest temperature that can be reached by evaporation of water from the wick around the WB thermometer. The amount of evaporation depends on the amount of water vapor in the air: the drier the air, the greater the evaporation and the greater the cooling. Another way of saying this is that the wet-bulb depression (T minus WB) will be greater if the air is drier. If the air is saturated, the maximum amount of water vapor is present and there is no evaporation and, therefore, no cooling. In this case, the wet bulb depression is zero.

Once dry bulb and wet bulb temperatures are measured, they are used to determine dewpoint temperature (T_d) and Relative Humidity (RH). These have been defined in Chapter 6 of *Aviation Weather*. In order to keep the important differences between T, T_d, WB, and RH clear, it is useful to review their definitions. In the space below, define the following terms.

1. Dry Bulb Temperature (T)

2. Wet Bulb Temperature (WB)

3. Dewpoint Temperature (T_d)

4. Relative Humidity (RH)

TASK 6-2: DEWPOINT AND RELATIVE HUMIDITY CALCULATIONS.

T_d and RH can be calculated directly or interpolated from tables. In this task, you will use the table method so you can easily observe the relation of RH to T and to WB. Use the appropriate table in Appendix C in *Aviation Weather*.

1. Determine WB depression, T_d, and RH for the data shown in table 6-1. There are some blank lines in the table for your own measurements if you have access to a psychrometer.

	T	WB	WB Depression	T_d	RH(%)
			TABLE 6-1		
a.	20°C	10°C	———— C°	———— °C	————
b.	80°F	70°F	———— F°	———— °F	————
c.	40°C	30°C	———— C°	———— °C	————
d.	0°F	–2°F	———— F°	———— °F	————
e.	105°F	65°F	———— F°	———— °F	————
f.	————	————	————	————	————
g.	————	————	————	————	————

2. Inspect your results in table 6-1. Note that in every case (if your answers are correct), one of the temperatures (T, WB, T_d) is always highest; one is always lowest; and the third is always intermediate. List them in decreasing magnitude for the general case. Under what conditions would all three be equal?

    a. Highest _____

    b. Intermediate _____

    c. Lowest _____

    d. All are equal when _____

3. Recall from the text that the part of the total atmospheric pressure exerted by the amount of water vapor present is called vapor pressure (VP). There is a theoretical upper limit to VP that depends on the temperature. This limit is

NAME: _____

DATE: _____ CLASS: _____

called saturation vapor pressure (SVP). Relative Humidity (RH) is simply the ratio between the two vapor pressures; that is,

$$RH(\%) = (\frac{VP}{SVP}) \times 100.$$

Table 6-2 shows the relationship between SVP and temperature. Use the equation above to compute the relative humidity for the temperature and dewpoint data given in table 6-3. Some blank spaces are provided in case you have made your determinations from your own psychrometric measurements. Indicate units where appropriate. Note: SVP is determined by using the dry bulb temperature (T) in table 6-2, while VP is determined by entering the same table with the dewpoint temperature (T_d). Your result in table 6-3, line a, should yield approximately the same RH that you have entered on the first line of table 6-1.

TABLE 6-2
SATURATION VAPOR PRESSURE OVER WATER

T (°C)	SVP (in. Hg.)	T (°C)	SVP (in. Hg.)
45	2.831	15	0.503
40	2.179	10	0.362
35	1.661	5	0.257
30	1.253	0	0.180
25	0.935	−5	0.124
20	0.690	−10	0.085

TABLE 6-3

a. T 20°C   SVP_____ T_d −1°C   VP _____   RH _____

b. T 0°C   SVP_____ T_d −10°C   VP _____   RH _____

c. T 30°C   SVP_____ T_d 29°C   VP _____   RH _____

d. T 26°C   SVP_____ T_d 20°C   VP _____   RH _____

e. T _____   SVP_____ T_d _____   VP _____   RH _____

f. T _____   SVP_____ T_d _____   VP _____   RH _____

TASK 6-3: METARS AND MOISTURE.

Temperature and dewpoint are commonly reported in METAR reports. Review your METAR code breakdown in Chapter 6 and Appendix D in *Aviation Weather*. Decode **ALL** temperature and dewpoint data in the following METAR reports. Place the information in table 6-4.

```
KMUO 070055Z 32013KT 30SM OVC070 13/M02 A2964 RMK PRESRR SLP037=
KMYL 070050Z AUTO 33004KT 10SM OVC060 07/M01 A2965 RMK AO2 SLP053 T00671006
 TSNO=
KU15 070048Z AUTO 29001KT 12/00 RMK AO1 T01220001=
KS80 062330Z 00000KT 20SM OVC030 10/05 RMK SLP072 NOSPECI T00950048=
```

TABLE 6-4

	Station Temperature (°C)	Dewpoint (°C)	Supplementary Temperature/ Dewpoint Data
KMUO	_____	_____	_____
KMYL	_____	_____	_____
KU15	_____	_____	_____
KS80	_____	_____	_____

TASK 6-4: WEATHER CHARTS, DEWPOINT, AND TEMPERATURE-DEWPOINT SPREAD.

Dewpoint and temperature-dewpoint spread are available on surface weather analysis charts and on constant pressure charts. These measurements, together with other moisture measures such as sky condition, weather, obstructions to vision, visibility, and radar reports, are useful tools for diagnosing and anticipating instrument conditions, icing, and some turbulence conditions. This task is designed to familiarize you with the charted data. Begin by answering the following questions.

NAME: _____

DATE: _____ CLASS: _____

1. In words, explain how the amount of water vapor in the air changes as the dewpoint temperature changes. (Hint: look at table 6-2)

2. Define "temperature-dewpoint spread."

3. In general, how is temperature-dewpoint spread related to relative humidity and saturation?

4. A portion of a surface weather analysis chart is presented in figure 6-2. Data plotted at individual stations is derived from METAR reports. In addition, lines of constant pressure (isobars) and fronts are also depicted. For this exercise, concentrate on dewpoint temperature and temperature-dewpoint spread. To help you interpret the data, a simplified "station plotting model" is included in the figure. For the stations within the numbered circles on the map, record the temperature and dewpoint data in table 6-5 and compute the temperature-dewpoint spread. **Be sure you indicate the correct units.**

5. Use Appendix C in *Aviation Weather* to compute the relative humidity for each station in table 6-5. Hint: You will have to use the temperature and dewpoint to determine the wet bulb depression in each case, then use the temperature and wet bulb depression to find relative humidity. Keep your temperature units consistent.

TABLE 6-5

Station Temperature	Dewpoint	Spread	Relative Humidity
1 _____	_____	_____	_____
2 _____	_____	_____	_____
3 _____	_____	_____	_____
4 _____	_____	_____	_____
5 _____	_____	_____	_____
6 _____	_____	_____	_____

NAME: _____

DATE: _____ CLASS: _____

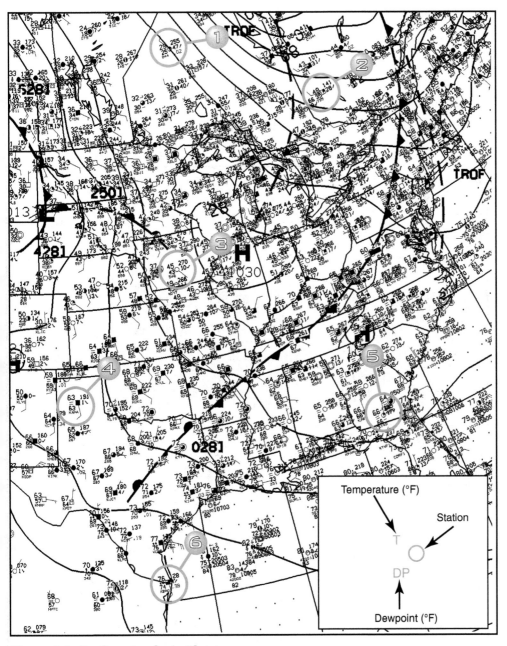

Figure 6-2. Surface Analysis Chart.

6. A portion of an 850 mb constant pressure chart is shown in figure 6-3. A simplified station plotting model is also included. Note that there are differences between the surface analysis and the constant pressure charts in the way dewpoint information is presented. Surface analysis charts show temperature and **dewpoint** in °F, while all constant pressure charts show temperature and **temperature-dewpoint spread** in °C.

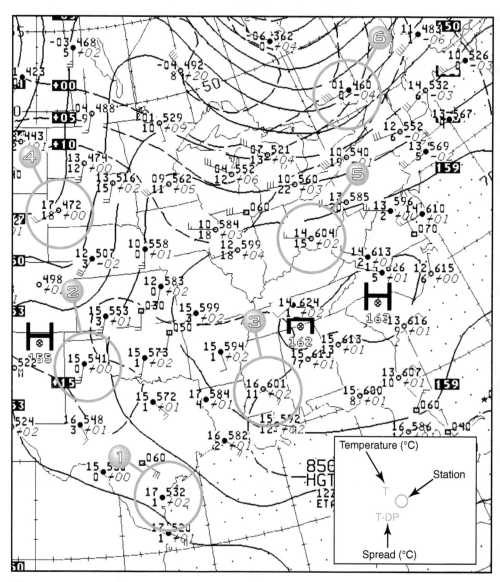

Figure 6-3. 850 mb Constant Pressure Chart.

NAME: _____

DATE: _____ CLASS: _____

In table 6-6, record the temperature and the spread, and compute the dew-point for the stations within the numbered circles in figure 6-3. **Indicate units.**

TABLE 6-6

Station	Temperature	Spread	Dewpoint
1	_____	_____	_____
2	_____	_____	_____
3	_____	_____	_____
4	_____	_____	_____
5	_____	_____	_____
6	_____	_____	_____

7. A temperature-dewpoint spread of zero indicates a relative humidity of 100% and the presence of a cloud. However, measurements of temperature and moisture made from a rising balloon are not instantaneous. When a sounding balloon passes quickly through a thin cloud layer or through the edge of a cloud, the spread will decrease, but not necessarily reach zero. Meteorologists have learned that wherever the temperature-dewpoint spread aloft is 5C° or less, there is a probability that a cloud layer is present. As the spread decreases to 3C° or less, the likelihood is that the layer is broken or overcast. To make the presence of cloud layers easy to see, the station circles on constant pressure charts are filled in whenever the spread is 5C° or less.* In figure 6-3, enclose the area(s) where the spread is 5C° or less with one or more solid curves. Shade the "cloudy" area(s) within the curve.

*CAUTION: This convention is NOT used on the surface analysis chart. A filled-in station circle at that level means that a cloud layer covering the sky has been observed, but it is not necessarily at the surface.

QUESTIONS

1. Complete the following statements:

   If the air is saturated, the relative humidity is _____% and the wet bulb temperature is (less than, equal to, greater than) _____ the air temperature which is (less than, equal to, greater than) _____ the dewpoint temperature.

   If the air is NOT saturated, the relative humidity is _____ % and the air temperature is (less than, equal to, greater than) _____ the wet bulb temperature which is (less than, equal to, greater than) _____ the dewpoint temperature.

2. On a calm, clear summer morning, the humidity will often be lower on the eastern side of a stone wall separating two pastures than on the western side. Thoroughly explain why this occurs.

3. (True, False) The dewpoint can be changed by evaporation. Explain.

NAME: _____

DATE: _____ CLASS: _____

4. A METAR observation reports a temperature/dewpoint as "20/20" but the relative humidity is not 100%. Is this possible? Explain.

5. Examine the temperatures and dewpoints in figure 6-2 to see if you can observe any connection between temperature-dewpoint spread and reports of visibility, cloud cover, and weather. Discuss.

EXERCISE 7:

CLOUDS

OBJECTIVES:
- To learn the standard procedures for observing and reporting sky condition and visibility
- To encode and decode METAR reports of sky condition and visibility

References: *Aviation Weather*, Chapter 6, "Atmospheric Moisture" and Appendix D, "Standard Meteorological Codes and Graphics for Aviation." Supplemental reading: *AC 00-45F, Aviation Weather Services*, Section 2.

BACKGROUND DISCUSSION

This exercise is a continuation of our examination of "the basics" of atmospheric moisture. Previously, you learned about certain measures of water vapor in the atmosphere such as dewpoint temperature and relative humidity. Now, we want to consider the results of condensation and deposition; that is, the formation of clouds and other obstructions to vision composed of water and ice particles.

The formation of clouds and fog results when air with adequate moisture and condensation nuclei is cooled to the dewpoint temperature. With continued cooling, excess water vapor changes state and forms liquid or ice particles. The resulting "visible moisture" has far-reaching effects on aviation including low ceilings, low visibilities, ice, and the decrease in stability caused by the release of latent heat. To help you understand these processes, several optional "kitchen" experiments related to cloud formation are included in the question section at the end of this exercise.

This exercise provides a practical look at the aspects of cloud and visibility observations including not only report decoding, but also how observations are made and how reports are encoded. With regard to the observed characteristics of clouds, sky condition refers to the state of the sky at the time of an observation (METAR) or terminal forecast (TAF). It is described by the five items listed in table 7-1.

TABLE 7-1. SKY CONDITIONS	
Cloud Type	Cloud category according to height and appearance.
Sky Cover	Amount of celestial dome hidden by clouds and/or obscurations. Figure 7-2 illustrates the **celestial dome.**
Summation Layer Amount	A categorization of the amount of sky cover at and below each reported layer.
Layer Height	The height (AGL) of the base of each reported layer of clouds and/or obscurations **above ground level** ; the vertical visibility into an indefinite ceiling.
Ceiling	The height **above ground level** of the lowest layer that is reported as broken or overcast; the vertical visibility into an indefinite ceiling.

As a pilot, you will be reading, listening to, and interpreting METAR reports. While being able to decode the reports is very important, their correct interpretation requires knowledge of how the observation is made and the report is written. There are certain subtleties that cannot be learned from decoding alone. When you read a METAR report, you must "stand in the shoes of the observer" to "see" what the observer sees. This exercise gives you some opportunities to do that.

Finally, the effect of the release of latent heat on stability during cloud formation will be examined. This effect can be treated as a simple extension of the previous exercise on stability in the dry atmosphere. The release of latent heat is critical in producing strong convection, especially thunderstorms.

TASK 7-1: CLOUD TYPES.

Clouds are generally classified according to their height and appearance. In the following, you will review cloud classifications.

1. Document the common height categories and height ranges of cloud bases in the following spaces. Also, list the names of the common cloud types in each height category.

NAME: _____

DATE: _____ CLASS: _____

Height Category	Height Range of Cloud Base (feet)	Cloud Types
Low Clouds	_____	_____
_____	_____	_____
_____	_____	_____

2. Certain cloud types are also known as "clouds with vertical development." List the clouds in this category.

3. Give examples of cloud types formed in a purely stable environment and those formed in a purely unstable environment.

Environment	Cloud Types
Stable	_____
Unstable	_____

4. Some cloud types appear to have a mixture of stability and instability influences. Name one of these cloud types and describe a realistic meteorological situation that could lead to the formation of the cloud type.

5. Write the dominant cloud type and likely height range (AGL) below each of the clouds in figure 7-1. Use your text as a guide. Be sure to look at both the cloud form and evidence of cloud height if available.

Figure 7-1. Cloud Identification.

NAME: _____

DATE: _____ CLASS: _____

TASK 7-2: SKY COVER: AMOUNTS, HEIGHTS, AND CEILINGS.

For reporting purposes, clouds are reported in **layers** where all cloud elements in the layer have bases at about the same height. The **amount** of sky cover for each layer is determined in eighths (octas) of the celestial dome. Cloud amounts for each layer are reported in categories that indicate how much of the sky is covered by the clouds and/or obscuring phenomenon. When interpreting cloud amount for a given layer, keep in mind that METAR weather observations are taken from the ground (or the tower); and the Summation Principle always applies; that is, sky cover at any level is the sum of the sky cover for the layer being evaluated and the sky cover of all lower layers including surface-based obscurations, such as fog, smoke, and dust.

This can be simply stated as the "at and below" rule: as observed from the ground, the cloud amount reported for any cloud layer is the sum of the amounts "at and below" that level.

1. To help you review the reportable categories of sky cover, define the following sky cover terms. Hint: review the METAR code breakdown in your text.

    Clear (CLR, SKC)   _____

    Few (FEW)   _____

    Scattered (SCT)   _____

    Broken (BKN)   _____

    Overcast (OVC)   _____

2. Define Ceiling

3. Define Indefinite Ceiling (VV)

4. Some examples of how sky cover is determined are shown in figure 7-2. This figure shows vertical cross sections of the celestial dome and the layer-by-layer cloud cover. The celestial dome is that portion (hemisphere) of the sky as seen by an observer standing on the earth. In each example, the observer stands at point "0." Cloud layers at various altitudes are indicated by irregular bands. The "pie-shaped" segments correspond to eighths of the celestial dome. The coded (METAR) sky cover is given at the bottom of the first three examples. Be sure that you understand why each case is coded as shown. Note, also, that the height of the ceiling is indicated in each report.

Write the correct METAR sky cover code for the three examples without coded reports in figure 7-2. Be sure to keep the Summation Principle (at and below) in mind. Cloud layers are coded sequentially from the ground up and coverage is cumulative. When multiple layers are present, no higher layer can be reported with less coverage than the layer below it. Indicate the ceiling where appropriate.

> **CAUTIONS: At an automated observation site, the reported sky cover is determined by a vertically pointing sensor that observes only those clouds immediately above the instrument. Furthermore, automated observations will not give information about clouds above 12,000 feet AGL. Also, remember that the METAR viewpoint is from the surface. Conditions will appear differently when observed in flight. METAR observations are taken more often (SPECI) when critical changes in ceiling and visibility occur. Always be sure that you have the latest weather information.**

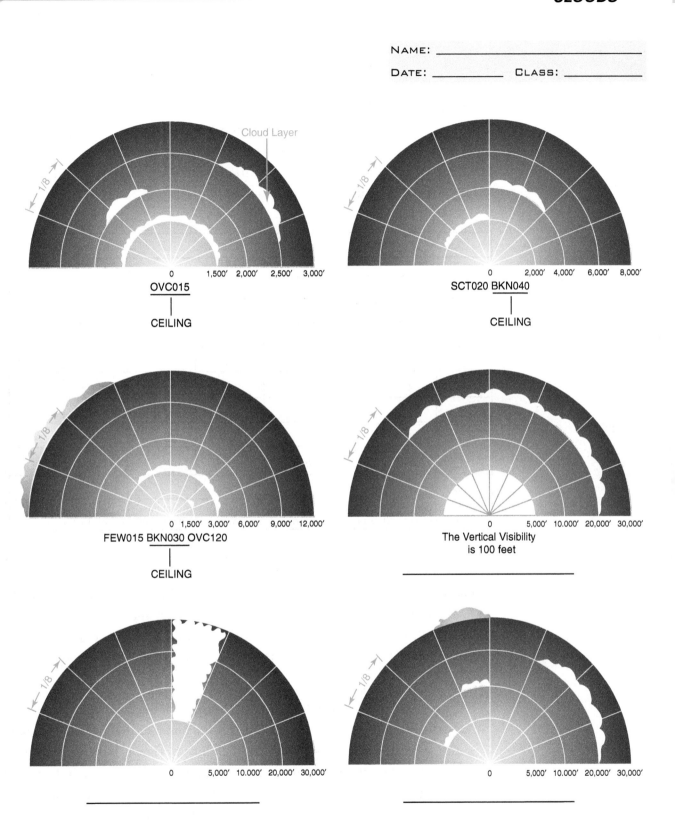

Figure 7-2. Sky Cover and the Celestial Dome.

TASK 7-3: VISIBILITY.

The interpretation of visibility information is key to understanding reported and predicted IFR conditions. This exercise conforms to the standard procedures used for manual observations. Only certain values of visibility are reported. These **reportable values** are given in table 7-2.

TABLE 7-2. REPORTABLE VALUES OF VISIBILITY (STATUTE MILES)							
Source of Visibility Report							
Automated			**Manual**				
M$^1/_4$	2	9[1]	0	$^5/_8$	1 $^5/_8$	4	12
$^1/_4$	2$^1/_2$	10	$^1/_{16}$	$^3/_4$	1$^3/_4$	5	13
$^1/_2$	3		$^1/_8$	$^7/_8$	1 $^7/_8$	6	14
$^3/_4$	4		$^3/_{16}$	1	2	7	15
1	5		$^1/_4$	1$^1/_8$	2$^1/_4$	8	20
1$^1/_4$	6[1]		$^5/_{16}$	1$^1/_4$	2$^1/_2$	9	25
1$^1/_2$	7		$^3/_8$	1 $^3/_8$	2$^3/_4$	10	30
1$^3/_4$	8[1]		$^1/_2$	1 $^1/_2$	3	11	35[2]

Note 1: These values may not be reported by some automated stations.
Note 2: Further values in increments of 5 statute miles may be reported, i.e., 40, 45, 50, etc.

Prevailing visibility is the greatest distance that can be seen over at least half of the horizon circle (not necessarily continuous). The **horizon circle** is illustrated in figure 6-13 in *Aviation Weather*. As a pilot, you must understand that the primary visibility reported in a METAR is the **prevailing visibility** and that the actual visibility in a particular direction near the reporting site may be lower.

1. Some examples of visibility observations are shown in figure 7-3. Consider these as "maps of horizontal visibility." North is at the top of the figure. The observer stands at the center of the circle and observes the indicated visibilities in each sector. The prevailing visibility is shown for the first three examples. Review the definition of prevailing visibility to be sure that you understand why it is the value given in the examples. Then, determine the prevailing visibilities for the six cases at the bottom of the page.

NAME: ____________________

DATE: __________ CLASS: __________

PREVAILING VISIBILITY

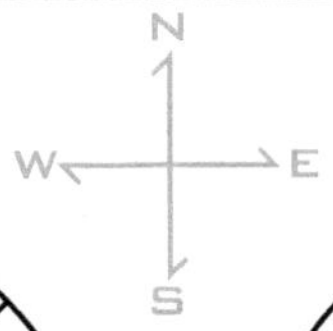
N
W
E
S

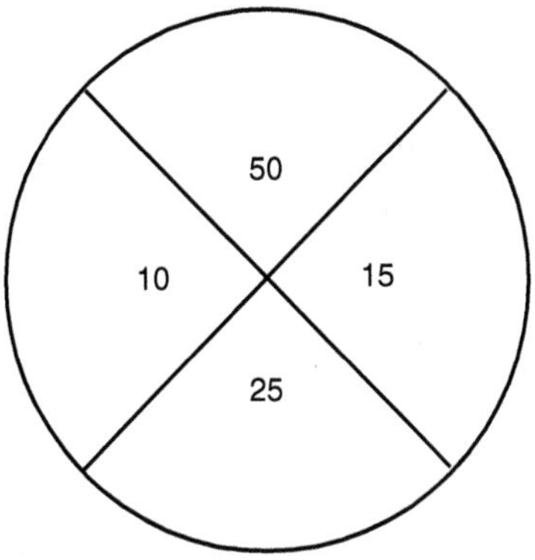
50
10
15
25

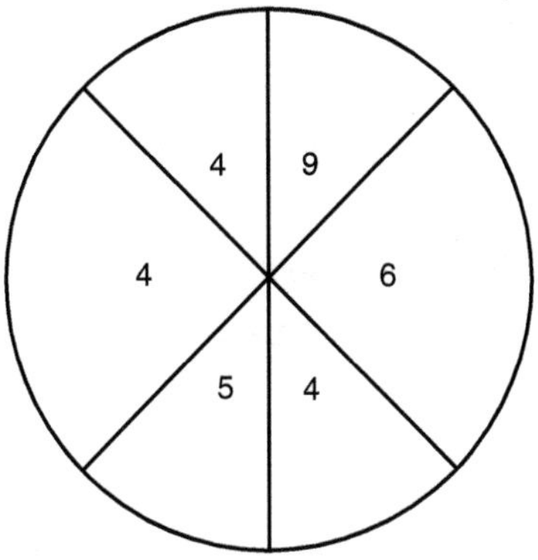
4
9
4
6
5
4

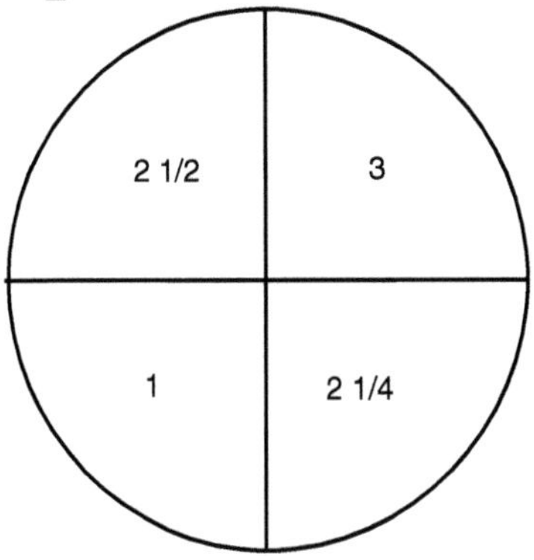
2 1/2
3
1
2 1/4

a. Prevailing Visibility 25 sm

b. Prevailing Visibility 5 sm

c. Prevailing Visibility 2 1/2 sm

Determine the following Prevailing Visibilities (sm).

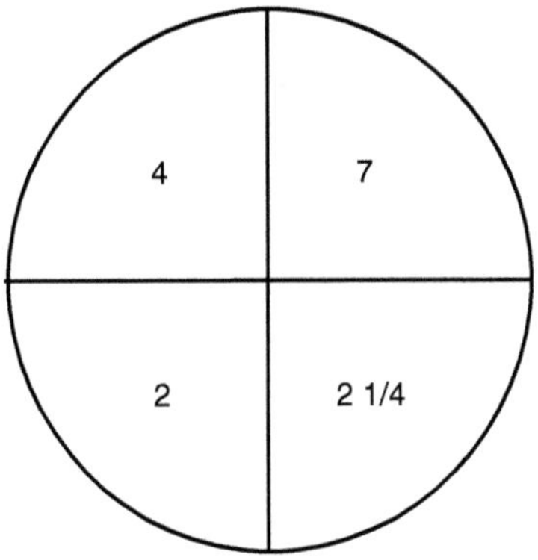
4
7
2
2 1/4

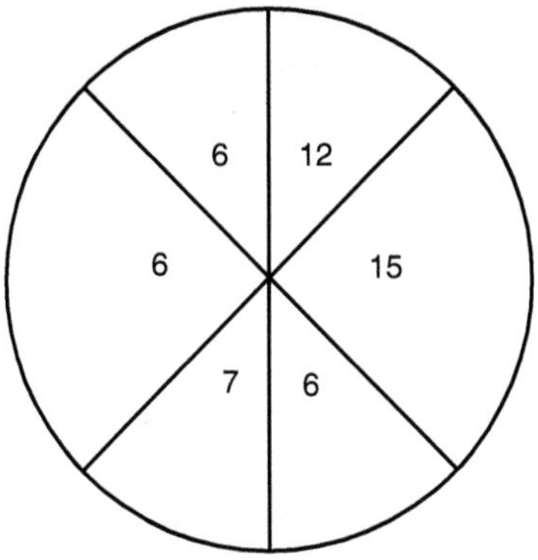
6
12
6
15
7
6

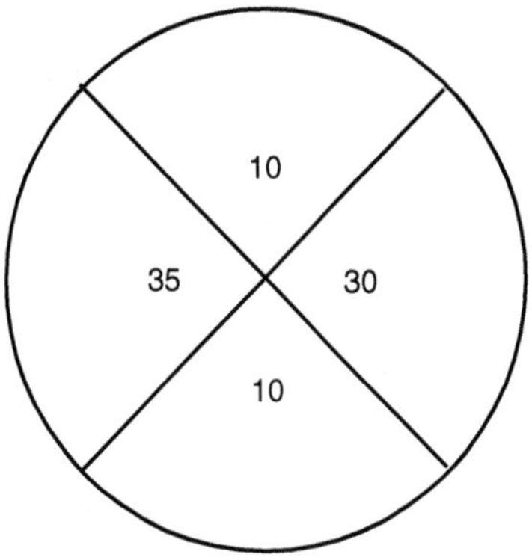
10
35
30
10

d. ____________________

e. ____________________

f. ____________________

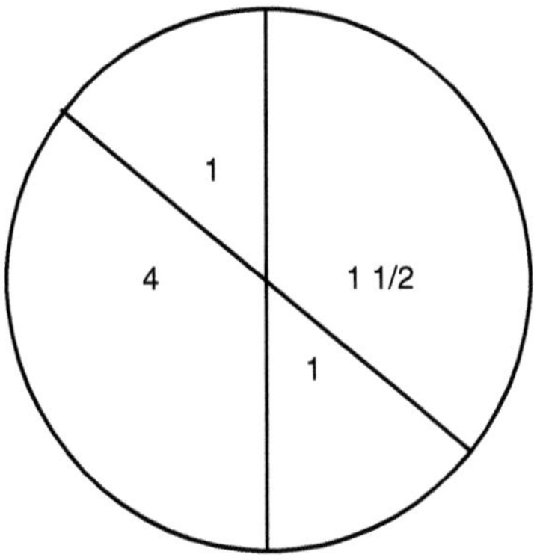
1
4
1 1/2
1

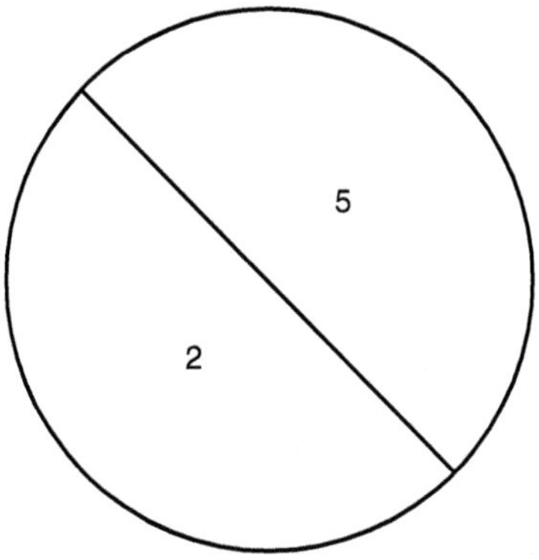
5
2

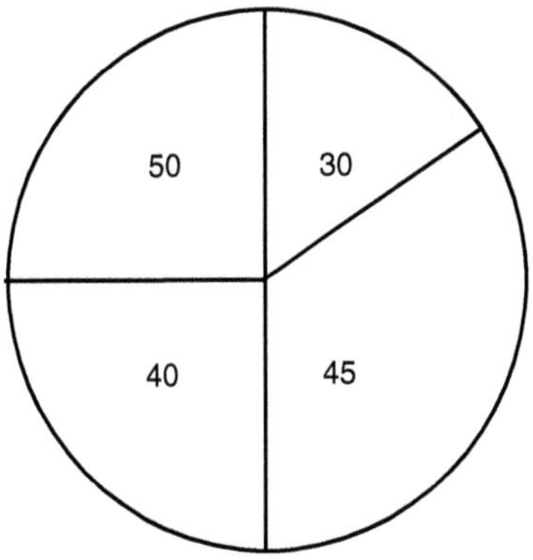
50
30
40
45

g. ____________________

h. ____________________

i. ____________________

Figure 7-3. Prevailing Visibility.

2. Sector visibility is the visibility in a specified compass direction (true direction) that represents at least a 45° arc (1/8th) of the horizon circle. Sector visibilities are shown in figure 7-3. At manual weather observation stations, **visibility in a particular sector is reported when that visibility differs from the prevailing visibility by more than one reportable value and either the prevailing visibility or sector visibility is less than three miles.** If these criteria are satisfied, the sector visibility will appear as a remark in the METAR report. Be aware that this is NOT the case for automated observation stations.

   Use the sector visibility reporting criteria given above and in table 7-2 to determine which of the nine examples in figure 7-3 will have sector visibility reported. Assume all reports are made at manual stations. Write the letter of the example(s) in the space below together with the appropriate remark for METAR.

Example	Prevailing Visibility (sm)	METAR Remarks
_____	_____	_____
_____	_____	_____
_____	_____	_____

3. **Flight Rules/Weather Reporting.** Give the ceiling and visibility criteria for the following conditions.

   VFR _____

   MVFR _____

   IFR _____

   LIFR _____

NAME: _____

DATE: _____ CLASS: _____

TASK 7-4: THE COMPLETE METAR CODE.

This task concludes your examination of METAR coding conventions. In later exercises, you will be expected to read and interpret METAR information with only occasional reference to the code breakdown. Begin by reviewing the METAR code for weather and obstructions to vision.

1. Define SPECI

2. Define AUTO

3. What is the difference between "mist" and "fog"?

4. What is the difference between "RA" and "SHRA"?

5. What is the difference between "prevailing visibility" and "runway visual range" in terms of the definition and METAR reporting format?

6. Four METAR reports are given below. Give **complete** plain language interpretations of each report in the space provided. Be sure to indicate the height of the ceiling, if one exists.

```
K3KM 081604Z AUTO 23017G23KT 1 1/2SM +RA BR SCT010 BKN017 OVC037 18/17 A2986
 RMK AO2 WSHFT 1540 PRESRR P0011 TSNO=

KIAB 081623Z 22009G21KT 4SM -SHRA BR FEW007 BKN010 OVC025 17/16 A2985 RMK
 PRESFR=

KICT 081556Z 21017KT 1SM +RA BR BKN012 BKN026 OVC050 18/17 A2985 RMK AO2 PK WND
 17026/1505 WSHFT 1458 SFC VIS 1 1/4 PRESRR SLP100 P0044 T01830172=

KDDC 081627Z 19021G26KT 10SM SCT012 BKN019 19/16 A2974 RMK AO2 PK WND 19032/1605=
```

K3KM

KIAB

NAME: _____

DATE: _____ CLASS: _____

KICT

KDDC

TASK 7-5: SATURATED CONDITIONS AND STABILITY.

When condensation or deposition occurs, latent heat is released. Since cooling is usually going on at the same time (in order to bring the air to saturation), the cooling is **partially** offset by the release of latent heat. This means that cooling will still occur, but at a slower rate. This process has a major impact on stability. The effect is easy to see if we redo a previous task from Exercise 5, and then introduce saturation to see the effect on the parcel stability. Table 7-3 shows a sounding from ground level to 5,000 feet AGL. Column A is the measured air temperature at each level.

1. **Dry Case.** At the indicated altitudes in table 7-3, compute the temperature of a parcel lifted from the surface to the specified level. Assume the parcel remains dry. Place the answers in column B. Put the computed differences between parcel and environmental (air) temperatures in column C. If the parcel is warmer than its surroundings, the difference is positive. If it is colder than its surroundings, the temperature difference is negative.

2. **Cloud Case.** Now, consider the case where the air parcel has enough water vapor to become saturated at exactly 2,000 feet AGL. That altitude is the base of the cloud **(condensation level)**. Above 2,000 feet, the rising parcel is saturated and latent heat is continuously released because of the condensation process.

   The cooling rate of a rising parcel below the cloud base is the dry adiabatic lapse rate (DALR). Above the cloud base, it cools at the saturated adiabatic lapse rate (SALR). Although SALR is less than DALR, SALR is **NOT a constant value**. At warm temperatures, where there is plenty of water vapor, large amounts of latent heat are released and SALR may be as small as 1C°/1,000 feet. At very cold temperatures, only small amounts of water vapor are available, latent heat release is small and SALR is only slightly less than DALR.

   In the Cloud Case given in table 7-3, compute the parcel temperatures again, but this time assume that the parcel is dry below 2,000 feet AGL and saturated at and above that level. Assume that the SALR is 2C°/1,000 feet (1C°/500 feet). Place your answers in column D. Compute the new difference between parcel and environmental air temperatures for each level. Place your answers in column E. Hint: you only need to recompute the parcel tem-

NAME: _____

DATE: _____   CLASS: _____

perature for the levels above the cloud base because the lapse rate up to the cloud base is the same for both the Dry Case and the Cloud Case.

3. Compare columns C and E in table 7-3. What do you conclude about the difference in stability between the Cloud Case and the Dry Case for a parcel lifted from the surface?

TABLE 7-3

		Dry Case		Cloud Case	
	A	**B**	**C**	**D**	**E**
Altitude	Air	Parcel	Difference	Parcel	Difference
Ft. AGL	$T_a°C$	$T_p°C$	$[T_p-T_a]C°$	$T_p°C$	$[T_p-T_a]C°$
0	12	——	——	——	——
1,000	7	——	——	——	——
2,000	4	——	——	——	——
3,500	2	——	——	——	——
4,000	2	——	——	——	——
5,000	4	——	——	——	——

QUESTIONS

1. A single, small fair-weather cumulus cloud is observed at your airport at 1 p.m. The cloud base is at 4,000 feet AGL. At 2 p.m., a layer of cumulus clouds at 4,000 feet AGL covers 1/8th of the sky. What would be the difference in the sky condition reports for the 1 p.m. and 2 p.m. METARs?

2. (True, False) An overcast layer is reported at 3,000 feet in the latest METAR. If you looked at the sky at the time and place of the observation, only about 1/8 of the overcast layer at 3,000 feet was visible, and a ceiling exists at a lower altitude. Explain.

3. What does the following visibility portion of a METAR report mean?

3/4SM R28R/2600FT

4. When any cloud forms, latent heat is released. As air continues to rise, the released heat reduces the rate of cooling due to expansion. All of these facts are true, yet stratiform clouds indicate that, in their case, the rising air is stable. Why doesn't the latent heat make the rising air unstable in this case?

5. The following are simple "kitchen" experiments that help explain the formation of clouds.

a. Fill a large bowl with ice. Set it on a table in a warm room. Darken the room and shine a flashlight across the bowl. Blow gently across the bowl. Describe and explain the cloud that forms. Describe an atmospheric phenomenon that is caused by a similar process.

b. Fill a large bowl with hot water. Put it in a cool environment (be careful with your refrigerator, you might ice it up!). Describe the cloud that forms. If you don't observe a cloud formation, the water-air temperature difference may not be large enough. If this is the case, darken the room and use a flashlight as in the first experiment. Explain the cloud formation. Describe an atmospheric phenomenon that is caused by a similar process.

c. This experiment requires a gallon jug (clear glass), a hand pump, a flashlight, a book of matches, and water. The pump should be attached through a stopper to the top of the jug so that air can be easily pumped into the jug without leaking out. (**CAUTION: only a small amount of pressurization is needed for this experiment. Use a simple hand pump. DO NOT use any type of pump that may dangerously over-pressurize the jug. Over pressurization may cause the glass jug to explode and cause serious injury.**) The attached pump should also be easily and quickly removable with the stopper. Place an inch or two of water in the bottom of the jug and perform the following experiments:

(1) Put the stopper in the jug and pump air into it. Only a small amount of pressurization is necessary for this experiment to work. Darken the room and shine a light through the jug. Pull the stopper. Describe the cloud that forms. If you have done the experiment correctly, there should be a very tenuous cloud in the jar. Explain the cloud formation and describe the role of all components of the apparatus and each step of the experiment.

(2) Light a match and drop it into the jug. Put the stopper in the jug and pump air into it. Darken the room and shine a light through the jug. Pull the stopper. Describe the cloud that forms. If you have done it right, there should be a more dense cloud than the previous experiment. Explain the denser cloud formation and describe the role of all components of the apparatus and each step of the experiment.

(3) After experiment (2), replace the stopper in the jug while the cloud is still visible. Pump air into the jug. What happens to the cloud? Explain.

EXERCISE 8:

METEOROLOGICAL SPACE AND TIME COORDINATES

OBJECTIVES:
- To familiarize you with map projections, coordinate systems, and map scales for weather maps
- To understand and use the basic time coordinate system used in operational meteorology

References: *Aviation Weather*, Appendix D, "Standard Meteorological Codes and Graphics for Aviation." Supplemental reading: *Guided Flight Discovery Private Pilot Manual*, Chapter 4, Section C, "Aeronautical Charts" and *AC 00-45F, Aviation Weather Services*, Sections 2, 4, and 6.

BACKGROUND DISCUSSION

Throughout this course and, later, when you apply your meteorological knowledge, you will be constantly exposed to weather maps. From these important graphic displays, you will determine current and future conditions along your planned flight track. As with navigational charts, the efficient use of weather maps starts with an understanding of the elements of map construction. Specifically, you must understand the concepts of map projection (how the nearly spherical earth is mapped on a flat surface), map coordinates (how position is uniquely specified on a given map), and map scale (the ratio of distance on the map to distance on the earth). The tasks you will complete here will give you practice in applying all of these concepts. But first, we will examine some mapping basics.

The construction of a flat map of the nearly spherical earth is not easy. There is always some type of distortion. For example, on some maps of the earth, a distortion in the relative size and shape of geographical features can occur. A comparison of Africa and Greenland is often a good example. The size of Greenland sometimes appears (erroneously) as large or larger than Africa.

Some distortions can be reduced, depending on just how the globe is projected onto the flat map. Map projection techniques are many and varied, depending on the intended use. The maps used in meteorology are carefully constructed to reduce distortions that can affect the accuracy of data, analyses, forecasts, and their interpretations. Some of the most common meteorological projections are Mercator, Polar Stereographic, and Lambert Conic. Geometric interpretations of these projections are illustrated in figure 8-1.

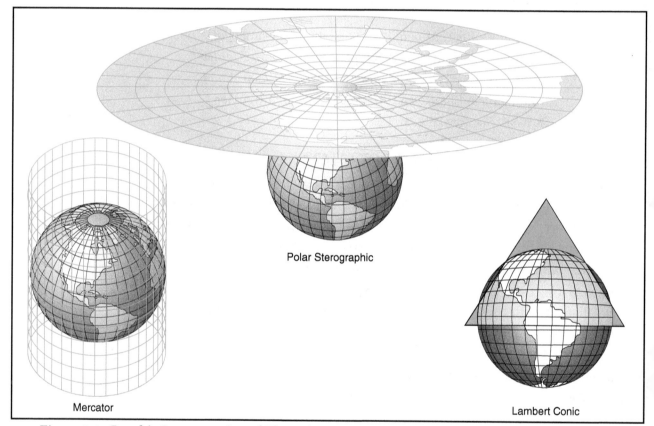

Polar Sterographic

Mercator

Lambert Conic

Figure 8-1. Graphic Interpretation of Three Common Map Projections.

All three of the map projections in figure 8-1 are conformal which means that,

1. at any point on the map, the map scale does not vary with direction **so angles are preserved** (this is important for representing wind directions accurately),

2. the shapes of relatively small geographic areas on the map correspond with their shapes on the globe, and

3. latitude and longitude lines intersect at right angles.

NAME: _____

DATE: _____ CLASS: _____

As you might expect, navigational charts are conformal in their construction. In fact, Lambert Conic and Mercator projections are commonly used for navigational charts. In the following tasks, you will use the global coordinate system on conformal charts to determine location and to estimate distances across the map. You will also examine evidence of distortion due to the projection. Finally, you will examine the time coordinate system commonly used in meteorology.

TASK 8-1: POSITION.

Every point on the earth is uniquely identifiable with its latitude and longitude position. Figure 8-2 depicts two diagrams of the globe. On the left, the earth is viewed from the North Pole (NP). On the right, the earth is viewed perpendicular to its axis so that the equator appears as a horizontal line.

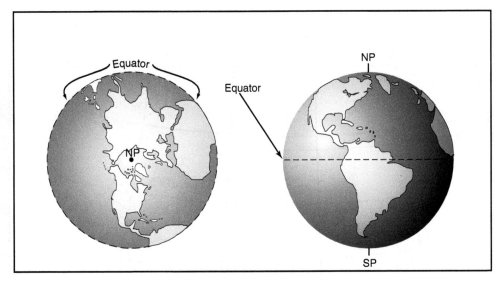

Figure 8-2. Global Latitude and Longitude.

1. On each diagram, draw lines that represent latitude (parallels) and longitude lines (meridians). Label the latitude and longitude lines that are great circles.

2. Although we look at latitude and longitude as coordinate "lines" on a map, they are actually "angles." In the space below, draw diagrams that clearly define how the latitude and longitude angles are determined.

3. Figure 8-3 is a map showing latitude and longitude, as well as state and national borders. Determine the latitudes and longitudes of the following points. Write your answers in the spaces provided (to the nearest °).

Point	Latitude	Longitude
1	_____	_____
2	_____	_____
3	_____	_____
4	_____	_____

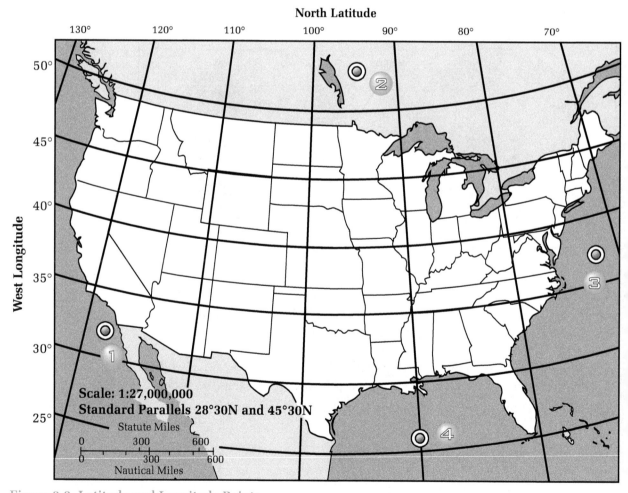

Figure 8-3. Latitude and Longitude Points.

NAME: _____

DATE: _____ CLASS: _____

Point	Latitude	Longitude	
⑤	46N	110W	
⑥	37N	94W	
⑦	28N	82W	
⑧	48N	124.5W	
⑨	_____	_____	Your Local Airport

4. Plot the location of the points listed above on figure 8-3. Label each point with a red dot and corresponding number.

5. (Optional) Place the state postal codes within the borders of each state in figure 8-3. Place the name of each of the Great Lakes within the border of each lake. Locate the Continental Divide.

6. (Optional) Figure 8-4 is the "Geographical Area Designator Map" showing area and terrain descriptors used by NWS (AC-0045). This terminology is very common in aviation weather forecasts. As a user of such information, you should be familiar with this nomenclature. On figure 8-4, draw a circle with a radius of 300 nautical miles around your local airport. In the following space, list all geographical designation terms applicable to the area within the circle.

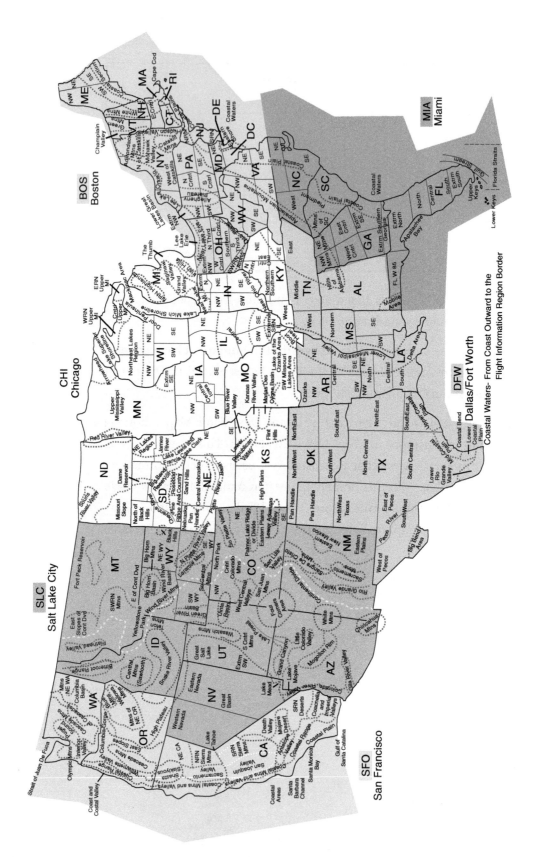

Figure 8-4. Geographical Area Designator Map. Shading corresponds to the Area Forecast (FA) regions.

NAME: _____

DATE: _____ CLASS: _____

TASK 8-2: DISTANCE.

Distance can always be estimated from a map if latitude and longitude grids are printed on the map. This is possible because each degree of latitude (N and S) is equal to 60 nautical miles. This is true for all latitudes with only a small error, which arises because the earth is not quite spherical. This tool is very useful for quickly approximating the size of atmospheric disturbances and the speed of movement and duration of storms.

Some of the problems of map distortion are minimized by using the "local latitude scale;" that is, by making a measurement of a particular distance with the latitude scale in the same vicinity. Of course, if there is a distance scale printed on the map, it can be used. You should be careful if only a single scale is given. In this case, the scale is only accurate for the "true" or "standard" latitude and there will be some map distortion elsewhere. The location of the standard latitude (there may be more than one) depends on the projection. For example, notice in figure 8-1 that the true latitudes are only where the projection intersects, or is tangent to, the globe. Some maps, such as a Mercator projection, get around the scale distortion problem by having a variable scale that is a function of latitude.

1. The latitude scale is appropriate for measuring distance, but the longitude scale (E and W) is not. Why?

2. What is the mathematical relationship between degrees of **longitude** and distance in nautical miles?

3. Knowing the distance between boundaries or geographical features on a map, such as state lines, is a useful resource for quickly estimating the dimension of weather systems. Use the local latitude scale on figure 8-3 to determine the North-South extent of the following features. Convert your measurements as indicated. (Optional) Check your answers with your flight computer.

One degree of latitude = _____ nm = _____ sm = _____ km

North-South Extent of Feature

	°Latitude	nm	sm	km
Oklahoma Panhandle	_____	_____	_____	_____
Florida	_____	_____	_____	_____
Lake Michigan	_____	_____	_____	_____
California	_____	_____	_____	_____
Vermont	_____	_____	_____	_____
Lower 48 States	_____	_____	_____	_____

4. Use the local latitude scale in figure 8-3 to estimate the distances between the following points to the nearest tenth of a degree. Convert to nautical miles. (Optional) Check your answers with your flight computer.

	° Latitude	nm
32N 120W and 40N 120W	_____	_____
32N 85W and 32N 95W	_____	_____

Note: The following questions refer to map scale.

5. What is the actual distance **on the map** between 25N and 30N in figure 8-3? Give your answer in either inches or centimeters.

   _____ in. or _____ cm

6. What is the actual distance between 25N and 30N on the earth? Convert the units.

   _____°Latitude = _____nm = _____in. or _____cm

7. Compute the approximate map scale for 25N to 30 N as (5) ÷ (6). Express as a ratio (1 ÷ some number) = _____ (Be sure your distances have the same units!)

8. (Optional) Compute the distance between 30N 90W and 45N 75W using the distance scale shown on the map, the local latitude scale and, if available, your flight computer. Explain the differences.

NAME: _____

DATE: _____ CLASS: _____

TASK 8-3: TIME COORDINATES.

In addition to spatial coordinates (latitude, longitude, and altitude), time coordinates are also critical. For example, meteorologists must coordinate the times of the worldwide weather observations and forecasts in order to meet the global requirements of modern aviation. Therefore, **ALL** times in operational meteorology are referenced to Coordinated Universal Time (UTC or Z), which is the local time adjusted to the 0° longitude line (the Prime Meridian). Observations, forecasts, weather maps, and charts are all identified with the UTC time. It is important to be able to convert UTC times to local times so that you can properly interpret weather information.

Since the earth rotates to the east at (approximately) one rotation every 24 hours and there are 360° of longitude around the globe, the clock is one hour earlier for each 15° of longitude west of Greenwich (Figure 8-2). The actual boundary of each one-hour time zone is not exactly parallel to the meridians in many areas due to political borders and local preferences. Also, many regions adopt daylight savings time for about half the year while others do not. Time zones are graphically shown in Chapter 17, Section B in *Aviation Weather*. In the following exercise, you will practice converting between various time coordinates.

1. Convert the following times to UTC.

    1200 PST   _____UTC

    4 p.m. CST   _____UTC

    0415 EST   _____UTC

2. Convert the UTC times below to the Local Standard Time (LST) or Local Daylight Time (LDT), as indicated.

    0215 UTC   _____ PST

    1654 UTC   _____ MST

    2359 UTC   _____ EST

    1030 UTC   _____ MST

    2120 UTC   _____ PDT

QUESTIONS

1. What two unique positions on the earth's surface are described only by their latitude?

2. How well do you know your geography? Without looking at a map, do the following mental exercise. Describe the countries and major water bodies along the 80W line of longitude. Start at the eastern part of Lake Erie and move southward to the South Pole. Hint: you will cross the U.S. Atlantic coast in South Carolina and just touch the southeastern coast of Florida. Check your answer with a map.

3. If you leave Seattle at 1700 PDT and reach Miami at 0700 UTC, what is your average ground speed? You should be able to estimate your answer without a flight computer. Can you do it?

4. What are the standard (true) latitudes in each of the projections in figure 8-1?

EXERCISE 9:

METEOROLOGICAL SATELLITE OBSERVATIONS OF ATMOSPHERIC CIRCULATIONS

OBJECTIVES:

- To introduce you to satellite imagery and its interpretation
- To examine the horizontal dimensions of various atmospheric circulations

References: *Aviation Weather*, Chapter 7, "Scales of Atmospheric Circulation."
Supplemental reading: *AC 00-45F, Aviation Weather Services*,
Section 3.

BACKGROUND DISCUSSION

With this exercise, we begin to apply the basic knowledge you have acquired to specific weather phenomena. To put our discussion in the proper perspective, it is useful at this point to introduce the concept of atmospheric circulation systems. These are more or less organized movements of air that produce other circulations and various weather phenomena. For example, a thunderstorm is a particular atmospheric circulation which can produce a tornado (another circulation) and hail (not a circulation, but certainly an important weather phenomenon). Knowing the characteristics of the circulations goes far in helping us understand weather.

There are many circulation systems in the earth's atmosphere. Some affect aircraft directly, while others are hardly felt. As with the thunderstorm and tornado, some circulations are embedded in others. The existence of some circulation systems is so fleeting that if you aren't paying attention, you may not know they are there. If they are important, you may be in trouble.

Scales of motion refers to the spatial and time (lifetime) dimensions that characterize each circulation system. The concept of scale is introduced here to help you organize the description and understanding of the atmospheric circulation systems that you will encounter during the rest of the course. At this point, it will be useful for you to review Chapter 7, Section A, in *Aviation Weather*.

In this exercise, you will first learn some basic properties and uses of meteorological satellite images. Then, you will identify a number of circulation systems using these images and conventional surface analysis charts.

TASK 9-1: SATELLITE IMAGES.

Figures 9-1 and 9-2 show GOES satellite images. GOES is a **G**eosynchronous **O**rbiting **E**arth **S**atellite. These satellites are put into an orbit directly over the equator at an altitude of about 22,000 miles. They orbit the earth at the same rate that the earth rotates, which allows each satellite to view the same area of the earth all of the time. The actual area viewed depends on the longitude of the satellite with each view extending from about 60°N to 60°S. The location of U.S. satellites depends on the number of operational GOES satellites in orbit. Often there is a "GOES West" satellite over the eastern Pacific and a "GOES East" over the western Atlantic. American polar-orbiting satellites and Asian and European geostationary satellites cover most of the rest of the earth. Figures 9-1 and 9-2 are from a GOES satellite that was located so it could view both the eastern Pacific and the western Atlantic.

Although the images in figures 9-1 and 9-2 were obtained at the same time and view the same area of the earth, they appear to be quite different. This is because the radiometer aboard the satellite sampled different parts of the electromagnetic spectrum. The image in figure 9-1 was viewed in the "visible" part of the spectrum. In this case, the satellite's radiometer measured **reflected solar radiation**. Remember that visible wavelengths dominate the electromagnetic spectrum of the sun (see figure 2-4 in *Aviation Weather*). Therefore, except for the fact that the image is in black and white, it appears much as we would see it from space with our own eyes. Appropriately, this is called a visible image. Notice that space appears black in a visible image.

The image in figure 9-2 was viewed in the "infrared" part of the spectrum. Recall that the earth and its atmosphere radiate their maximum energy in the infrared (IR) part of the electromagnetic spectrum because their temperature is low compared to the sun (see figure 2-4 in *Aviation Weather*). Although gases such as water vapor and carbon dioxide tend to absorb IR radiation, the radiometer is designed to sense a narrow band within the IR part of the spectrum that is not affected by the presence of IR-absorbing gases. From that information, it is relatively easy to determine the radiating temperature of clouds and the earth's surface. The temperature of these features can vary greatly depending on latitude, ground cover, ground elevation, and the altitude of the cloud tops. We call the map of those temperature features an IR image. The convention for IR images is to display the temperature as shades of gray, ranging from very black (warm) to

NAME: _____

DATE: _____ CLASS: _____

GOES-7 1 OCT 92 AT 18:01 UTC

Figure 9-1. GOES Visible Image.

very white (cold). Space appears white (cold) in an IR image. Note also that the resolution of features in the IR image is typically less than a visible image.

You may see a number of variations in satellite images. For example, the "full disk" images are often "sectorized" to produce regional views more suitable for local applications. You also may see color versions of IR images, where colors are arbitrarily assigned to different temperature ranges. There are many different color and black and white combinations that meteorologists use for a variety of reasons. Also, you occasionally may see images generated in radiation channels other than IR and visible, which are used to examine different characteristics of the earth and the atmosphere. The most common, however, are visible and infrared images such as those shown in figures 9-1 and 9-2. Answer the following questions by referring to those figures.

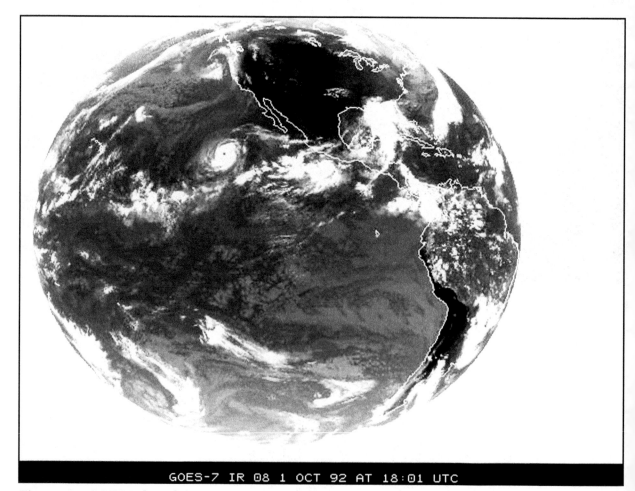

GOES-7 IR 08 1 OCT 92 AT 18:01 UTC

Figure 9-2. GOES Infrared Image.

NAME: _____

DATE: _____ CLASS: _____

1. What local times were the images obtained?

   EST _____ CST _____ MST _____ PST _____ HST _____

2. Notice that the appearance of the cloud free area of the North American continent is fairly homogeneous in the visible image, but portions of the west appear significantly darker in the IR image than in the visible image. Give a reasonable explanation for this difference.

3. In the visible image, there are many clouds off the West Coast of South America. However, in the IR image, those clouds can hardly be distinguished. Give a reasonable explanation for this difference.

4. On the basis of your answers in **1** and **2**, which radiometer channel is useful during daylight hours? _____ Which radiometer channel returns useful data 24 hours a day? _____

5. The tops of the clouds within the circle at position 1 in figure 9-1 are at two or more different levels. Explain how you can reach this conclusion (hint: look at the IR image in the same area).

6. Common cloud features on satellite images include vortexes, commas, bands, clusters, and cells. Circle and label one of each of these features on figure 9-1.

TASK 9-2: EVIDENCE OF ATMOSPHERIC CIRCULATIONS.

1. The satellite images of figures 9-1 and 9-2 show evidence of several apparent circulations of very different scales. As discussed in Chapter 7 of *Aviation Weather*, the largest scale atmospheric circulation is the general circulation. Evidence of a feature of the general circulation is found in the intertropical convergence zone (ITCZ). In figures 9-1 and 9-2, the ITCZ appears as a broken line of convective clouds that stretches from Central America across the Pacific toward the western edge of the image. Circle and label the ITCZ on each image.

2. The presence of another circulation is evident in the swirl of clouds off the West Coast of the U.S. This is an extratropical (ET) cyclone, a disturbance that develops and moves along the polar front (another feature of the general circulation). The organized cloud vortex, which marks the location of the extratropical cyclone, is best seen in the visible image in figure 9-1. The infrared image, in figure 9-2, shows just a faint "footprint" of the circulation since only the brightest (highest and coldest) clouds are obvious. Circle the ET cyclone and label it on both images. Notice that the horizontal extent of the ET cyclone is much smaller than the ITCZ.

3. Another obvious, but still smaller scale, circulation is the tropical cyclone located over the Western Pacific between southern Mexico and the Hawaiian Islands. The cyclone is identified by a tight cloud vortex and a distinct "eye." Examine both images. Notice that the tropical cyclone appears to be smaller in the IR image. This is because lower and warmer clouds involved in the low-level circulation are not clearly distinguished in the IR image. Another small-scale tropical vortex that is in the developing stages can be identified in the visible image, just off the coast of Central America. Circle and label both tropical cyclones on figures 9-1 and 9-2. If you have already circled one of these in a previous task, simply identify it with a second label.

4. The smallest scale circulations that are evident in the satellite images are best seen in figure 9-1. Across the image, small white dots of "popcorn" appear at all latitudes. This is evidence of convection. The dots are clusters of cumuliform clouds or the tops of thunderstorms (CB). The circulation in these clouds is vertical; that is, air rises in the clouds and sinks in the surrounding clear air. You can tell that much of the convection is restricted to lower levels because the cloud tops in most of the convective areas of figure

NAME: _____

DATE: _____ CLASS: _____

9-1 do not show up clearly in figure 9-2. Exceptions are found in the ITCZ and over South America where the cold, high anvils associated with individual thunderstorms can be seen in both the visible and the IR images. Circle the area of thunderstorms over South America and label it clearly.

5. Estimate the horizontal dimensions of the ITCZ, extratropical cyclone, the largest of the tropical cyclones, and one of the thunderstorms that you identified in the last four tasks and enter your answers in table 9-1. You can use various geographical features as rough "measuring sticks." For example, the length of Baja, California is about 600 nautical miles and, along the Pacific Coast, the distance from the Mexican Border to the Canadian border of the U.S. is about 1,000 nautical miles.

6. Surface weather analysis charts show wind and pressure fields from which organized circulations can be directly identified. A surface analysis chart is given in figure 9-3. Note the high and low pressure areas labeled 1 through 3. As you know, in the Northern Hemisphere, winds circulate counterclockwise around lows and clockwise around highs. These are examples of large-scale, organized atmospheric circulations. The low pressure area labeled 1 is an extratropical cyclone. Recall that it develops outside of the tropics. In contrast, the low pressure area labeled 3 is a tropical cyclone that develops at low latitudes. This particular tropical cyclone has reached the most intense form, known in this area as a "hurricane."

Determine the horizontal dimension of each of these circulations as the length of the heavy blue line through the center of the circulation. This measurement is only approximate since the shapes and intensities of the circulations are not necessarily symmetrical. Use the latitude scale of the map to make an approximate measurement. Be careful with map distortion. Enter your answers in table 9-1.

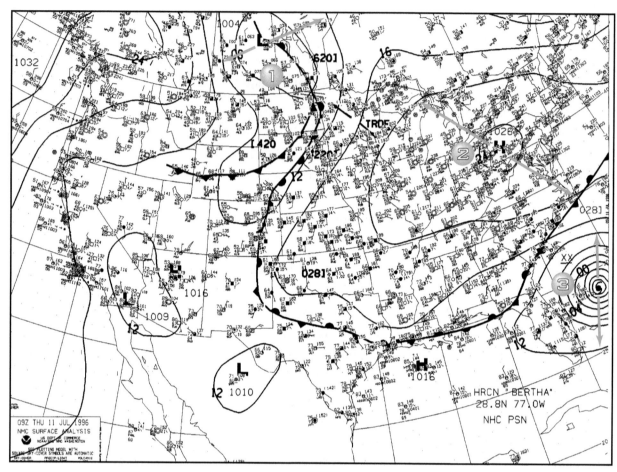

Figure 9-3. Surface Weather Analysis.

7. Estimates of the sizes of the smallest scale circulations will be based on your own observations. For example, you have probably seen a "dust devil;" that is, a rapidly rotating column of air that becomes visible as it picks up dust and debris. This is not a tornado. It is a weaker circulation that often develops over very hot surfaces under clear skies at the hottest time of day. In table 9-1, write an estimate of the diameter of a dust devil that you have seen.

NAME: _____

DATE: _____ CLASS: _____

8. If you have seen a tornado, even in a photograph or a film, write your estimate of its diameter in table 9-1.

TABLE 9-1
HORIZONTAL SCALES OF OBSERVED CIRCULATIONS

Circulation (Name)	Scale (°Lat.) (optional)	Scale (nm)	Rank	Time to cross at 100kts (hours)
Source: Satellite Images (Figures 9-1 and 9-2)				
ITCZ	_____	_____	_____	_____
ET Cyclone	_____	_____	_____	_____
Tropical Cyclone	_____	_____	_____	_____
Thunderstorms	_____	_____	_____	_____
Source: Surface Weather Analysis Chart (Figure 9-3)				
ET Cyclone (Low)	_____	_____	_____	_____
Anticyclone (High)	_____	_____	_____	_____
Tropical Cyclone	_____	_____	_____	_____
Source: Visual Observations				
Tornado	_____	_____	_____	_____
Dust Devil	_____	_____	_____	_____

QUESTIONS

1. In table 9-1, rank the circulations from the smallest (rank 1) to the largest.

2. In table 9-1, compute the time it would take you to fly across each circulation at a constant ground speed of 100 knots.

3. Plot your results along the vertical axis on the left side of figure 7-1 in *Aviation Weather*. Discuss. Do your answers agree or disagree with the text? If they disagree, why?

4. Use figure 7-1 to estimate the range of the typical lifetimes of each of the circulations you have listed (in days and hours).

5. (Optional) Go online to the AWC URL at http://aviationweather.gov/

   In the web site menu, under "Observations," click on "Satellite." You will be given choices of displays according to weather satellite imagery (visible, infrared, etc.) and region of interest.

   Click "Infrared (B/W)" for the latest black and white satellite image for the "Contiguous U.S." Note the image date and time and the cloud and temperature distributions (black warm/white cold). If possible, print out the image.

   Repeat the process, but this time select "Infrared (Color)" for the contiguous U.S. Again, note the date and time of the image. Be sure the Color and B/W images are less than an hour apart. Compare the clouds and temperatures (red warm/blue cold).

   Which map gives you the most useful information at a glance? Why?

EXERCISE 10:

AIRMASSES, FRONTS, AND EXTRATROPICAL CYCLONES: SURFACE WEATHER ANALYSIS

OBJECTIVES:

- To familiarize you with the typical structure of an extratropical cyclone in the lower troposphere
- To help you identify extratropical cyclone features using weather maps and reports

References: *Aviation Weather*, Chapter 8, "Airmasses, Fronts, and Cyclones" and Appendix D, "Standard Meteorological Codes and Graphics for Aviation." Supplemental reading: *AC 00-45F, Aviation Weather Services*, Section 4.

BACKGROUND DISCUSSION

An extratropical (ET) cyclone is an atmospheric disturbance found in **midlatitudes**. In contrast, tropical cyclones develop in **low latitudes**. From an aviation point of view, an ET cyclone is a "storm" in every sense of the word. Most of the known aviation weather hazards can occur in the ET cyclone. These include low ceilings and visibilities, icing, gusty surface winds, thunderstorms, wind shear, and clear air turbulence (CAT). A thorough understanding of the cyclone structure will help you learn where and why these hazards occur. In this exercise, we examine the ET cyclone structure near the surface. In the next exercise the structure in the mid- and upper troposphere is considered.

Extratropical cyclones are large, low-pressure areas. These cyclones are typically a few hundred to several hundred miles in diameter, and they go through identifiable stages of development in the days between their initial appearance and their dissipation. To understand the developmental process, it is helpful to have a good grasp of the structure and behavior of a "typical" or "average" ET cyclone. The average characteristics are generally referred to as the polar front model. This model was determined from detailed observational studies. The model is presented in figures 8-10 and 8-11 in *Aviation Weather*. This model is very useful in estimating the whole ET cyclone structure, given only sparse data. The polar front model of the ET cyclone also serves as a useful forecast tool.

As discussed in *Aviation Weather*, ET cyclones develop and move along the polar front. A front is a boundary between cold and warm **airmasses**. The cyclone develops as an incipient wave-shaped disturbance on the polar front. The wave, with its apex at the center of the low, intensifies rapidly over the next 12 hours. It then enters the occluded stage, as the cold front overtakes the warm front. Thereafter, the ET cyclone gradually weakens and dies over the next few days. During this time, the low generally moves eastward or northeastward at a speed of 20 knots in the early stages, markedly slowing down as it occludes. It is important to keep in mind that, during the lifetime of the ET cyclone, cold and warm airmasses and their associated fronts are carried around the cyclone in a counterclockwise circulation (Northern Hemisphere) while the cyclone moves toward the east.

In summary, the most important components of the ET cyclone in the lower troposphere are:
- two or more <u>airmasses</u>
- <u>fronts</u>
- a distinct region of <u>low pressure</u> with a well defined cyclonic* circulation
- organized <u>cloud and precipitation areas</u>
  * counterclockwise in the Northern Hemisphere

In the following tasks, you will examine data and surface maps for evidence of these features. You will identify airmasses, construct isobars, and locate the cloud and precipitation shield. In addition, you will document frontal characteristics from METAR data.

NAME: _____

DATE: _____ CLASS: _____

TASK 10-1: AIRMASSES.

Airmasses are classified as "cold" if the air is colder than the ground, and "warm" if the air is warmer than the ground. Cold and warm airmasses each have unique weather conditions. Cold airmasses typically have good visibilities, but they are often unstable and more turbulent than warm airmasses, especially near the ground. If there is adequate moisture present, cumulus clouds occur with the possibility of showers and locally reduced visibility, thunderstorms, turbulence, and low-level gustiness. Warm airmasses tend to be stable with reduced visibilities due to smoke and haze. If there is adequate moisture, fog and low ceilings often form, especially at night.

As discussed in *Aviation Weather*, cold airmasses are usually identified as **Polar** or **Arctic** to reflect their source region. Warm airmasses are often **Tropical**. An airmass source region is an area with very homogeneous surface conditions and typically dominated by high pressure systems. Winds are light in these circulations, and the air remains over the area for long periods of time. This allows the air to adapt itself to the surface temperature and moisture conditions. High latitude areas of ice and snow and the warm oceanic areas in low latitudes are often airmass source regions.

When an airmass leaves its source region, it is modified by the surfaces over which it moves. For example, within several days, a cold, dry airmass moving over an oceanic region will warm up significantly and gain moisture. Also, when an airmass moves over a snow-free land area, the diurnal heating and cooling of the surface causes both warm and cold airmasses to be less stable during the day and more stable at night. You can identify cold and warm airmasses by examining the reported temperatures on a map. For example, true Arctic air is identified by temperatures of 0°F (–18°C) and below. Polar airmasses are somewhat warmer with typical winter temperatures between 10°F to 40°F (–12°C to 4°C). Dewpoint temperatures are particularly useful in identifying moist, tropical air where dewpoints are greater than, or equal to, 60°F (16°C). In the present task, you will use these elementary guidelines to identify airmasses on a surface weather analysis chart.

1. Examine the temperature variations across the map in figure 10-1 and place a red "W" at the location of the warmest temperatures in the warm airmass(es) and a blue "C" at the location of the coldest temperatures in the cold airmass(es). There may be more than one of each.

2. Do you find any Tropical air on the map? If so, label its center with a red "T."

3. Do you find any Arctic or Polar air on the map? If so, label the center(s) with a blue "A" and/or "P."

TASK 10-2: FRONTS.

Fronts are often the focus of bad flying weather. This frontal weather is in addition to any poor flying conditions that may be generated within the airmasses. Fronts are narrow zones of transition between different airmasses. The zones are typically a few tens to a few hundred miles wide. An aircraft penetrating a front will experience not only weather but also temperature, pressure, and wind changes. Gusty surface winds and low-level wind shear conditions occur along fronts. Turbulence is not unusual. Because fronts are lifting mechanisms (see Exercise 5), low ceilings and visibilities, thunderstorms, precipitation, and icing are common when adequate moisture is present. Since you have already identified at least two different airmasses in Task 1, you know that one or more fronts must also be located on the map, somewhere between the centers of the airmasses. In this task, you will refine those positions to reveal some important characteristics of fronts.

Examine the temperatures over the areas **between** the centers of the cold and warm airmasses in figure 10-1. Look especially for areas where temperatures change rapidly over relatively short distances. The actual frontal zones will be found somewhere in these areas.

1. Analyze the temperature field in figure 10-1 by drawing red lines of equal temperature (isotherms) at 5F° intervals. The 40°F isotherm has been drawn on the map to get you started. Neatly label the value of each isotherm where it reaches the edge of the map. (For more guidance in analysis, refer to Exercise 2, Task 2-4.)

2. The frontal zone is the elongated region where the isotherms are close together. Other ways of saying this are: "the temperature changes rapidly across the frontal zone;" or "the frontal zone is a region where the temperature gradient is strongest." Shade the estimated position of the frontal zone lightly in blue.

3. **Type of Fronts.** Ordinarily, fronts are identified over a sequence of analyses. This approach is particularly important when identifying occluded or stationary fronts. Cold and warm fronts are easier to identify on a single surface chart, especially if they are strong and rapidly moving. In a cold front, cold air is replacing warm air. Therefore, you will find the winds blowing toward the front in the cold air. Crossing from the cold side of the front to the warm side, it is common to find a wind shift in the frontal zone from west or northwest winds in the cold air to south or southwest winds in the warm air.

NAME: _____

DATE: _____ CLASS: _____

With a well-defined warm front, the winds blow toward the warm front in the warm air. The wind shift is usually from southerly winds (SW-SE) on the warm side of the frontal zone to easterly winds (SE-NE) on the cold side. The map in figure 10-1 has a warm and a cold front. By convention, both warm and cold fronts are drawn along the **warm** sides of the frontal zones. Place heavy dashed lines along those boundaries as your first estimates of the frontal positions. Inspect the winds near the dashed lines and identify the frontal types using the guidelines on wind directions given above. Label the fronts clearly as "warm" or "cold."

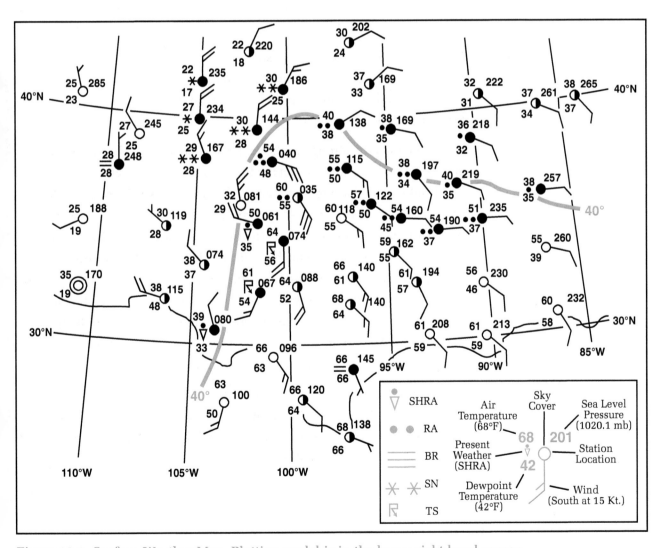

Figure 10-1. Surface Weather Map. Plotting model is in the lower right hand corner.

TASK 10-3: PRESSURE FIELD.

The construction of the pressure field will complete your analysis of the surface weather map using the polar front model as a guide. The examination of the pressure field contributes three important pieces of information to your airmass and frontal analyses.

- It isolates the major circulation features on the map, including extratropical cyclones and high pressure regions
- It defines the general features of the entire wind field
- It provides independent evidence of frontal locations

1. On figure 10-2 (identical to 10-1), draw lines of constant pressure (isobars) at 4 mb intervals. The 1020 mb isobar has been drawn on the map to help you get started. Label the isobars clearly with their individual values.

2. Neatly transfer the estimated positions of the fronts (dashed lines) from figure 10-1 to figure 10-2. **Important Note:** the point on the map where the warm and cold fronts join must be at the point of lowest pressure in the center of the main low-pressure system on the map.

3. In the vicinity of strong fronts, isobars often display bends or "kinks," emphasizing that fronts are usually found in pressure troughs. This structure is caused by the sharp temperature difference across the front. It is the reason why the wind direction shifts significantly in the vicinity of a front and why the pressure usually falls as the front approaches and rises as the front passes. If the cold front you have drawn falls outside a nearby pressure trough, it is not located properly. In this case, recheck the nearby winds and temperatures. The trough associated with a warm front is frequently difficult to find because the frontal zone is broader and the associated temperature gradient is weaker than a cold front. In this case, winds, weather, and temperatures are better indicators of the frontal position.

4. After you are sure that your fronts are in the correct locations, use correct color codes and symbols shown in table 10-1 to draw the final warm and cold front positions on figure 10-2. Be sure they agree with the temperature, wind, and pressure information on the chart.

NAME: _____

DATE: _____ CLASS: _____

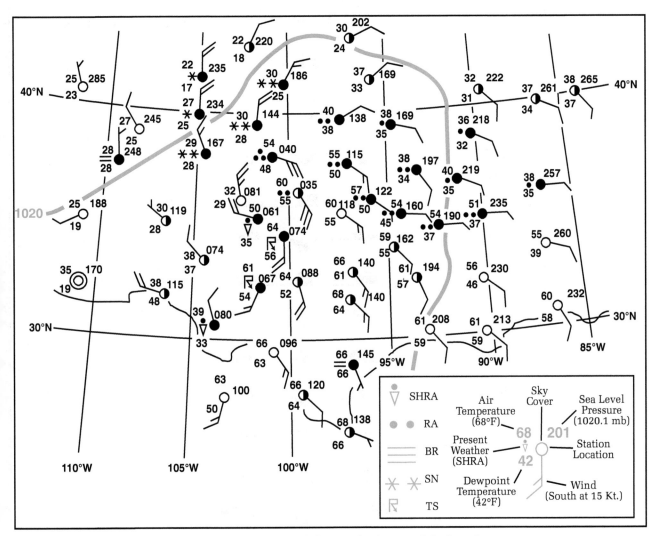

Figure 10-2. Surface Weather Map. Plotting model is in the lower right hand corner.

TABLE 10-1

COLOR	SYMBOL	DESCRIPTION
Blue	H	High Pressure Center
Red	L	Low Pressure Center
Blue	▼▼▼	Cold Front
Red	⌒⌒⌒	Warm Front
Red/Blue	⌒ ▼ ⌒	Stationary Front
Purple	⌒ ▲ ⌒	Occluded Front
Blue	▼ ▼ ▼	Cold Frontogenesis
Red	⌒ ⌒ ⌒	Warm Frontogenesis
Red/Blue	⌒ ▼ ⌒	Stationary Frontogenesis
Blue	▼ — ▼	Cold Frontolysis
Red	⌒ — ⌒	Warm Frontolysis
Red/Blue	⌒ — ▼ — ⌒	Stationary Frontolysis
Purple	⌒ — ▲ — ⌒	Occluded Frontolysis
Purple	— •• — •• —	Squall Line
Brown	— — — —	Trough Line (TROF)

NAME: _____

DATE: _____ CLASS: _____

TASK 10-4: PRECIPITATION PATTERNS.

The precipitation shield is the organized region of precipitation caused by frontal lifting and the general upward motions resulting from the extratropical cyclone. Surface heating, orography, and small-scale convergence and divergence may modify the idealized patterns shown in *Aviation Weather*, and discussed here.

1. On figure 10-2, use a thick dark line to enclose the area of the map where precipitation is occurring.

2. Shade the shower and thunderstorm symbols in red. Note the tendency for precipitation to be organized in a relatively narrow band behind the cold front.

3. Shade the steady precipitation symbols in green. Notice the tendency for clouds and precipitation to be organized in a relatively broad band along and ahead of the warm front.

TASK 10-5: FRONTAL PASSAGE.

Four sequences of METAR data are given below. If necessary, review the METAR code in Appendix D of *Aviation Weather*. Either a warm or a cold front passed the station during each sequence. The fronts were not particularly strong and, in some cases, were very slow moving so that the reporting station was in the frontal zone for some time. Upon close inspection, the reports reveal the changes in pressure, temperature, wind, and weather associated with each frontal type. For each sequence, in the spaces provided,

1. determine when and what type of front has passed.

2. in plain language, list the METAR information that supports your answer. (Hints: look at **changes** in wind, temperature, pressure, and weather information. Depending on the strength and type of front and the time of its passage, the change in temperature due to the change in airmasses may be masked by radiational heating or cooling. In these cases, look at the 24-hour temperature change.)

```
KPDT 230456Z 07013KT 10SM FEW070 BKN080 OVC110 06/03 A2975 RMK AO2 RAE54 PRESFR
    SLP075 P0004 T00610028=
KPDT 230556Z 09007KT 10SM BKN080 OVC095 07/03 A2973 RMK AO2 SLP065 60005
    T00720028 10072 20028 58020=
KPDT 230656Z 06011KT 10SM OVC090 07/03 A2969 RMK AO2 PRESFR SLP049 T00720028=
KPDT 230756Z 13005KT 10SM OVC095 08/02 A2971 RMK AO2 WSHFT 0713 SLP055
    T00830017 401060000=
KPDT 230856Z 10018G26KT 10SM -RA OVC060 08/01 A2969 RMK AO2 PK WND 11026/0848
    RAB54 SLP051 P0000 60000 T00830011 56018=
KPDT 230956Z 10011KT 10SM OVC075 08/02 A2967 RMK AO2 RAE12 SLP045 P0000
    T00830017=
KPDT 231056Z 09004KT 10SM -RA OVC070 09/03 A2966 RMK AO2 RAB49 SLP042 P0000
    T00890028=
KPDT 231156Z 14010KT 10SM FEW070 OVC090 11/02 A2966 RMK AO2 RAE04 SLP042 P0000
    60000 70005 T01060022 10106 20067 56014=
KPDT 231256Z 21010KT 10SM OVC095 11/03 A2967 RMK AO2 SLP047 T01060028=
KPDT 231356Z 30010KT 5SM BR OVC100 04/03 A2971 RMK AO2 SLP061 T00390033=
KPDT 231456Z 31006KT 6SM BR FEW120 03/03 A2972 RMK AO2 SNB20E23 SLP068 P0000
    60000 T00280028 53022=
KPDT 231556Z 35007KT 4SM BR BKN065 04/03 A2975 RMK AO2 SLP075 T00390033=
KPDT 231656Z 05006KT 8SM -RA OVC050 06/04 A2974 RMK AO2 RAB34 SLP071 P0000
    T00560039=
```

Frontal passage at _____ UTC

Type of Front _____

Evidence:

NAME: _____

DATE: _____ CLASS: _____

KMEM 091751Z 13008KT 1 1/2SM BR OVC002 10/09 A2972 RMK DZB14E39 SLP063 60000
 T00970094 10097 20048 58020=
KMEM 091851Z 18008KT 2SM BR OVC002 11/10 A2969 RMK SLP052 T01070103=
KMEM 091950Z 18009KT 5SM BR OVC003 12/11 A2966 SLP044 T01190113=
KMEM 092051Z 19008KT 7SM BKN009 OVC015 13/12 A2965 RMK SLP 040 T01290115 56022=
KMEM 092151Z VRB005KT 7SM OVC011 13/12 A2965 RMK SLP040 T0133011=
KMEM 092251Z 14006KT 5SM BR BKN013 OVC031 13/12 A2964 RMK SLP036 T0130116=
KMEM 092351Z 11006KT 8SM OVC014 13/12 A2962 RMK SLP030 T01320121 10133 20097
 58010=
KMEM 100051Z 15005KT 7SM OVC010 14/13 A2960 RMK SLP023 T01350126=
KMEM 100151Z 18006KT 7SM -RA BKN007 OVC100 14/14 A2958 RMK RAB01 SLP016
 T01390135=
KMEM 100250Z 20008KT 6SM BR BKN007 OVC019 15/15 A2960 RMK RAE06 SLP023 60002
 T01520146 55007=
KMEM 100350Z 21010KT 8SM -RA SCT013 BKN030 OVC100 16/15 A2959 RMK RAB11 SLP019
 T01590147=
KMEM 100451Z 20009KT 170V240 8SM -RA SCT010 BKN070 OVC100 16/15 A2957 RMK
 SLP012 T01580147=
KMEM 100510Z 29012G23KT 240V320 8SM BKN006 OVC070 16/15 A2958=
KMEM 100523Z 28009G23KT 10SM -RA SCT005 OVC049 14/11 A2958=
KMEM 100552Z 26009KT 20SM FEW070 13/10 A2958 RMK RAE04B19E35 SLP015 60001
 T01330100 10161 20133 401610047 55007=
KMEM 100652Z 32010KT 7SM BKN005 OVC070 13/12 A2958 RMK SLP015 T01270120=
KMEM 100752Z 24011KT 7SM FEW005 12/11 A2960 RMK SLP021 T01170109=
KMEM 100852Z 26014K 10SM BKN011 10/08 A2964 RMK SLP035 T00990079 53020=
KMEM 100952Z 27014KT 12SM OVC013 09/06 A2967 RMK SLP047 T00870064=
KMEM 101051Z 26010KT 10SM SCT018 OVC027 08/06 A2970 RMK SLP057 T00810059=
KMEM 101152Z 29012G18KT 12SM OVC014 08/05 A2973 RMK SLP068 70001 T00780053
 10133 20078 52030=
KMEM 101250Z 30010G20KT 15SM OVC021 07/04 A2977 RMK SLP082 T00690038=
KMEM 101351Z 30009KT 20SM SCT014 OVC026 07/04 A2980 RMK SLP090 T00680041=
KMEM 101451Z 29010KT 250V350 20SM BKN013 OVC020 07/04 A2984 RMK SLP103
 T00660040 51036=
KMEM 101550Z 30015G20KT 20SM BKN017 OVC035 07/03 A2986 RMK SLP111 T00670026=
KMEM 101651Z 32014G20KT 20SM OVC020 06/02 A2990 RMK SLP125 T00580016=
KMEM 101750Z 30011G17KT 20SM OVC017 05/01 RMK SLP125 T00470007 10078
 20047 51020=

Frontal passage at _____ UTC

Type of Front _____

Evidence:

```
KJAN 091754Z VRB04KT 5SM BR OVC007 17/16 A2976 RMK AO2 SLP074 T01720156 10172
  20133 58010=
KJAN 091854Z VRB04KT 5SM BR OVC009 18/16 A2974 RMK AO2 SLP069 T01780161=
KJAN 091954Z VRB04KT 5SM OVC011 18/17 A2971 RMK AO2 SLP058 T018300167=
KJAN 092054Z VRB05KT 5SM BR OVC012 19/17 A2970 RMK AO2 SLP055 T01890172 56018=
KJAN 092154Z 16004KT 6SM FEW018 OVC024 19/17 A2970 RMK AO2 SLP055 T01940172=
KJAN 092254Z 14005KT 4SM BR FEW018 17/16 A2969 RMK AO2 SLP052 T01720161=
KJAN 092354Z 13005KT 4SM BR OVC024 17/17 A2969 RMK AO2 SLP052 T01720167 10194
  20161 58004=
KJAN 100054Z 13007KT 5SM BR FEW022 SCT029 BKN085 17/17 A2968 RMK AO2 SLP050
  T01720167=
KJAN 100154Z 14009KT 4SM BR FEW005 SCT037 BKN070 17/17 A2968 RMK AO2 SLP047
  T01720167=
KJAN 100221Z 14012KT 2SM +RA BR SCT013 BKN049 OVC100 17/17 A2967 RMK AO2 RAB14
  P0008
KJAN 100228Z 14012KT 3SM -RA BR FEW006 BKN026 OVC065 17/17 A2966 RMK AO2 RAB14
  P0008
KJAN 100254Z 24009G16KT 4SM BR SCT005 BKN020 OVC025 18/18 A2967 RMK AO2
  RAB14E31 SLP043 P0008 60008 T01780178 58010=
KJAN 100354Z VRB05KT 4SM BR BKN007 OVC012 19/18 A2965 RMK AO2 CIG 005V010
  PRESFR SLP036 T01890183=
KJAN 100454Z 24006KT 4SM BR BKN007 BKN010 OVC028 19/18 A2967 RMK AO2 RAB22E54
  CIG 004V009 SLP044 P0003 T01890183=
KJAN 100554Z 26007KT 7SM OVC065 18/17 A2968 RMK AO2 SLP049 60011 T01830167
  10194 20167 401940122 53008=
KJAN 100654Z 26009KT 10SM BKN075 17/14 A2970 RMK AO2 SLP055 P0001 T01720139=
KJAN 100754Z 24003KT CLR 14/11 A2972 RMK AO2 SLP062 T01440111=
KJAN 100954Z 23004KT CLR 12/10 A2974 RMK AO2 SLP069 T01220100=
KJAN 101054Z 00000KT CLR 11/09 A2975 RMK AO2 SLP073 T01060094=
KJAN 101154Z 26005KT CLR 11/08 A2977 RMK AO2 SLP079 T01110078
  10183 20094 53013=
KJAN 101254Z 27008KT 10SM 11/06 A2980 RMK AO2 SLP091 T01110056=
KJAN 101354Z 30010G15KT 10SM CLR 11/04 A2984 RMK AO2 PRESRR SLP104 T01110044=
KJAN 101454Z 33008KT 10SM CLR 10/06 A2986 RMK AO2 SLP111 T01000061 51033=
KJAN 101554Z 31009KT 10SM CLR 10/05 A2989 RMK AO2 SLP121 T01000050=
KJAN 101654Z VRB04KT 10SM BKN026 11/06 A2992 RMK AO2 SLP129 T01110061=
KJAN 101754Z 27009KT 10SM BKN026 12/06 A2991 RMK AO2 SLP 126 T01170056 10117
  20100 50014=
```

Frontal passage at _____ UTC

Type of Front _____

Evidence:

NAME: _____

DATE: _____ CLASS: _____

KCHS 091756Z 00000KT 3SM BR OVC012 12/11 A2991 RMK AO2 SLP129 T01220106 10122
  20072 58019=
KCHS 091856Z 00000KT 3SM BR BKN008 OVC014 13/11 A2990 RMK AO2 SFC VIS 4 SLP123
  T01330111=
KCHS 091956Z 36003KT 3SM BR OVC017 13/12 A2990 RMK AO2 SFC VIS 5 SLP124
  T01330117=
KCHS 092056Z 32005KT 3SM BR FEW010 OVC015 13/12 A2992 RMK AO2 SFC VIS 5 SLP131
  T01330122 55000=
KCHS 092156Z 35004KT 3SM BR SCT008 OVC015 13/12 A2994 RMK AO2 SFC VIS 4 SLP136
  T01280117=
KCHS 092256Z 36006KT 3SM BR FEW008 OVC019 12/11 A2994 RMK AO2 SFC VIS 6 SLP136
  T01170111=
KCHS 092356Z 03003KT 3SM BR OVC010 11/11 A2997 RMK AO2 SFC VIS 6 CIG 008V011
  SLP146 T01110106 10139 20111 53016=
KCHS 100056Z 03006KT 3SM BR OVC013 11/11 A2995 RMK AO2 VIS 5 SLP141
  T01060106=
KCHS 100156Z 36003KT 3SM BR BKN004 OVC011 11/11 A2997 RMK AO2 SFC VIS 4 SLP147
  T01060106=
KCHS 100256Z 00000KT 3SM BR OVC004 11/11 A2998 RMK AO2 SFC VIS 4 CIG 003V006
  SLP150 T01060106 53004=
KCHS 100356Z 02004KT 2 1/2SM BR OVC004 11/10 A2998 RMK AO2 TWR VIS 3 SLP151
  T01060100=
KCHS 100456Z 05004KT 1 3/4SM BR OVC002 11/10 A2996 RMK AO2 TWR VIS 3 SLP144
  T01060100 401390061=
KCHS 100556Z 07005KT 1 1/2SM BR OVC002 11/10 A2993 RMK AO2 TWR VIS 3 SLP134
  T01060100 10111 20100 58015=
KCHS 100656Z 08006KT 3/4SM BR OVC002 11/11 A2990 RMK AO2 TWR VIS 3 PRESFR
  SLP123 T01060106=
KCHS 100756Z 09003KT 1SM BR OVC002 11/11 A2986 RMK AO2 TWR VIS 3 PRESFR SLP109
  T01110106=
KCHS 100856Z 12005KT 3SM -RA BR OVC002 11/11 A2984 RMK AO2 RAB55 SLP103 P0000
  60000 T01110111 56033=
KCHS 100956Z 09009KT 1 3/4SM RA BR BKN002 BKN028 OVC035 12/12 A2980 RMK AO2 TWR
  VIS 3 PRESFR SLP090 P0008 T01170117=
KCHS 101056Z 11011KT 2SM RA BR BKN002 OVC018 13/12 A2975 RMK AO2 TWR VIS 3
  PRESFR SLP074 P0013 T01280122=
KCHS 101156Z 14010KT 3SM BR BKN002 OVC019 14/14 A2975 RMK AO2 SFC VIS 5 RAE36
  PRESFR SLP073 P0005 60026 70026 T01440139 10144 20106 56028=
KCHS 101256Z 15008KT 3SM -RA BR BKN004 BKN013 OVC017 16/16 A2975 RMK AO2
  RAB05E35B53 SLP073 P0000 T01610156=
KCHS 101356Z 19010KT 3SM BR BKN009 BKN014 19/18 A2972 RMK AO2 SFC VIS 4 RAE02
  CIG 006V013 PRESFR SLP065 P0000 T01890183=
KCHS 101456Z 21017KT 6SM BR BKN007 BKN011 OVC034 21/19 A2971 RMK AO2 RAB30E52
  SLP060 P0002 T02060194=
KCHS 101556Z 22010KT 6SM BR OVC009 21/19 A2972 RMK AO2 CIG 006V012 SLP065
  T02060194=
KCHS 101656Z 20011KT 7SM BKN010 OVC015 21/19 A2969 RMK AO2 SLP055 T02110194=
KCHS 101756Z 26009G16KT 8SM BKN015 BKN022 23/19 A2968 RMK AO2 SLP049 60002
  T02280194 10228 20144 58010=

Frontal passage at _____ UTC

Type of Front _____

Evidence:

QUESTIONS

1. You are flying westward at 7,000 feet AGL in the warm air ahead of a cold front that is oriented north-south. Describe the wind, weather, and temperature changes as you fly through the front into the cold air.

2. In question 1, how would your altimeter setting change to maintain a true altitude of 7,000 feet?

3. In question 1, how far west of the surface position of the front would you encounter the front at 7,000 feet? (Assume that the surface is at sea level.)

4. ET cyclones tend to move toward the (direction) _____ while, initially, tropical cyclones tend to move toward the (direction) _____.

NAME: _____

DATE: _____ CLASS: _____

5. A strong cold front moves rapidly across west Texas. Extensive dust clouds make the front visible. There are no other clouds. Explain.

6. The lower structure of fronts moving across mountainous regions is often poorly defined. Why?

7. Obtain a series of surface maps from the World Wide Web. (See *Aviation Weather, 3rd Edition*, Appendix F.) Identify the stage of development and speed of movement of any ET cyclones shown on the maps. Also estimate the speed of various types of fronts.

EXERCISE 11:

TROUGHS, RIDGES, AND EXTRATROPICAL CYCLONES: UPPER AIR ANALYSIS

OBJECTIVES:
- To familiarize you with the structural components of the extratropical cyclone in the middle troposphere
- To help you identify extratropical cyclone features using weather maps and satellite images

References: *Aviation Weather*, Chapter 8, "Airmasses, Fronts, and Cyclones" and Appendix D, "Standard Meteorological Codes and Graphics for Aviation." Supplemental reading: *AC 00-45F, Aviation Weather Services*, Sections 3 and 4.

BACKGROUND DISCUSSION

This exercise is a continuation of our study of ET cyclones. Now we examine the structure of those disturbances in the mid-troposphere. Fronts are not ordinarily indicated on upper air meteorological charts; rather, lows, highs, troughs, ridges, and jet streams receive attention.

On a constant pressure chart, a trough is an elongated region of relatively low heights. If it is located properly, heights will increase as you move away from the trough line (the axis of the trough). A ridge is an elongated region of relatively high heights. If it is located properly, heights will decrease as you move away from the ridge line (the axis of the ridge). As shown in the schematic drawing in figure 11-1, ridges and troughs are usually found together. They are visible in the wave-like patterns of contours and isotherms. Upper lows, highs, and wave disturbances are common at all latitudes. However, in this exercise, we will focus on the disturbances in the midlatitudes, particularly those associated with ET cyclones.

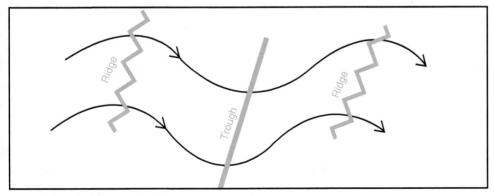

Figure 11-1. Schematic of wave pattern in contours on a constant pressure chart. Arrowheads have been placed on the contours to indicate approximate wind direction. Lower heights are on the left, looking downwind. Distance between ridges (wave length) is typically 1,000 nautical miles or more.

The ET cyclone structure aloft differs markedly from low-level conditions you saw in the last exercise. Winds strengthen and often change direction with height above the surface, which can impact navigation, fuel economy, and safety. Knowledge of the complete model of the ET cyclone will help you deal with these problems whether you are reading about the current or forecast weather, interpreting weather maps or satellite images, or receiving a briefing.

The life cycle of an ET cyclone aloft often parallels the behavior of the cyclone at the surface. As shown in figure 11-2, the wave trough grows in amplitude and forms a closed circulation aloft. This occurs about the time the surface low (if present) occludes. Also, the upper-level trough line aloft usually lags behind (to the west) of the surface low-pressure system in the early stages and catches up to it during occlusion. This structure is illustrated in *Aviation Weather*, figures 8-12 and 8-13. This phase relation between the surface cyclone and the upper air trough produces mass divergence near the tropopause ahead (east) of the trough line. The divergence, in turn, causes the pressure to fall rapidly at the surface during the development stage of the surface low.

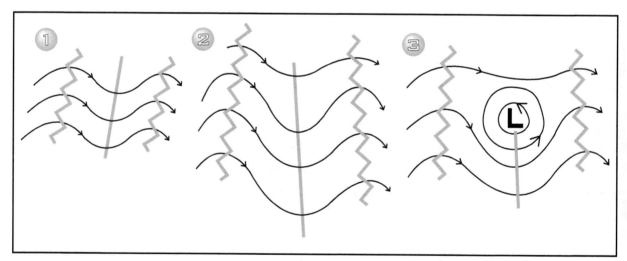

Figure 11-2. Development of a trough into a more intense, closed circulation aloft. The time between the first and the third diagram is 12 to 24 hours. During this intensification period the trough is moving eastward. Its speed typically decreases as it intensifies.

In the following tasks, you will review the information found on constant pressure charts, identify wave disturbances aloft on both constant pressure charts and satellite images, and link this information to the surface structure of an ET cyclone.

NAME: _____

DATE: _____ CLASS: _____

TASK 11-1: DATA AND ANALYSIS REVIEW.

A 500 mb constant pressure analysis chart is shown in figure 11-3. Use this figure to answer the following questions.

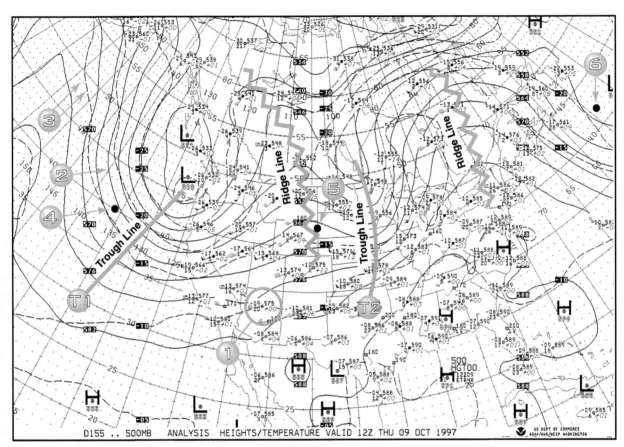

Figure 11-3. 500 mb Constant Pressure Chart for 9 October 97, 1200 UTC.

1. Decode the information plotted at the station labeled ① and place your answers in the following spaces. Be sure to indicate units.

   Temperature _____, Height _____, Wind Direction _____,

   Wind Speed _____, Temperature-Dewpoint Spread _____.

2. The standard height of this constant pressure surface is _____ feet _____meters MSL.

3. The line indicated by the single arrow at point ② is a line of constant _____ or a(an) _____.

4. The line indicated by the double arrow at point ③ is a line of constant _____ or a(an) _____.

5. At which point is the wind the strongest? ④ , ⑤ , or ⑥ _____. Explain.

TASK 11-2: IDENTIFICATION AND MOVEMENT OF WAVE DISTURBANCES ALOFT.

As discussed in Chapter 8, Section A of *Aviation Weather*, ET cyclones show up aloft as both closed lows and wave-like structures in the contours and isotherms. Both are important weather producing features. The closed lows are easily identifiable, but the wave disturbances require some practice.

Figure 11-3 has two wave disturbances identified by trough lines T1 and T2. Notice that each of these disturbances is centered on the wave trough in the contours and is flanked by ridges. These ridge lines are also identified. The following are some important properties of wave troughs aloft:

- Wave disturbances have a range of wave lengths from a few hundred nautical miles to several thousand nautical miles. Those with wave lengths of about 1,000 nautical miles are particularly important weather producers.

- Wave disturbances and closed lows have much longer lifetimes than the time between constant pressure charts (12 hours), so they are usually identifiable from one map to another.

- Wave disturbances commonly move more slowly than the strongest westerly winds in their vicinity; in fact, the longer the wave, the slower the movement.

- A "typical" wave aloft moves at about 25 knots or about 600 nautical miles per day.

- Closed lows move more slowly than wave disturbances and may become stationary for long periods, especially when they are cut off to the south of the main jet stream.

1. Figure 11-4 shows the 500 mb conditions 24 hours after the chart in figure 11-3. In figure 11-4, find the T1 and T2 wave troughs in their new locations. Remember, the troughs will be downstream (to the east) of their earlier positions in figure 11-3. Draw a heavy line in the new position of each trough line and label them T1 and T2, respectively. (See the symbols for trough lines in figure 11-3.)

2. Locate, draw, and label the flanking ridge lines for each trough. (See the symbols for ridge lines in figure 11-3.)

3. Transfer the **original** positions of the **trough lines** from figure 11-3 to figure 11-4 so you can graphically see the 24-hour trough movement.

4. Compute the speed of movement of each trough line in knots and place your answers in table 11-1.

NAME: _____

DATE: _____ CLASS: _____

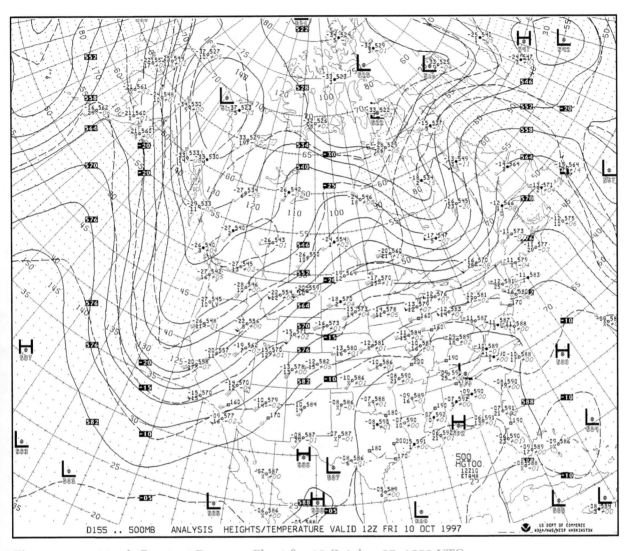

Figure 11-4. 500 mb Constant Pressure Chart for 10 October 97, 1200 UTC.

TABLE 11-1.		
Trough	24–hour Movement (nm)	Speed (kts)
T1	_____	_____
T2	_____	_____

TASK 11-3: CLOUDS AND WEATHER ASSOCIATED WITH UPPER LEVEL DISTURBANCES.

Deteriorating weather typically forms on the downwind or **bad weather side** of troughs, while improving conditions are typical of the upwind side. Downwind in the westerlies is toward the east.

1. On figure 11-3, lightly shade (in pencil) the area between each trough line and the **downstream** ridge line. Do not obliterate any data; you will need it later. This is a rough approximation of the region of bad weather (ET cyclone development, clouds, precipitation) associated with each trough at the time of the chart.

2. The cloudy area between the trough and downstream ridge also may be used to estimate the bad weather area. It can be found indirectly by inspecting the reports of temperature-dewpoint spread on constant pressure charts. Where the spread is 5C° or less, there is a high probability that a scattered or greater cloud layer exists at that level. For this task, you will use the "5° spread rule" to estimate cloud cover at the 500 mb level. On figure 11-3, lightly shade (in green) those stations where the spread is 5C° or less **within the continental U.S.** Recall that the stations reporting these values have a station circle that is black.

3. You know from Exercise 9 that satellite images show **total sky cover** viewed from above. Figures 11-5 and 11-6 are infrared images from the GOES West and GOES East satellites. The images were obtained within 30 minutes of the time of figure 11-3. The IR imagery is presented here because it emphasizes the higher, colder clouds (whiter) characteristic of wave disturbances aloft. In figures 11-5 and 11-6, respectively, trough lines T1 and T2 have been superimposed on the images. Also, the center of the closed low on the northwest coast of the U.S. has been located on figure 11-5.

   a. Transfer the positions of the flanking ridge lines for troughs T1 and T2 in figure 11-3 to the satellite images in figures 11-5 and 11-6. Label each clearly as "ridge line." Notice the position of the extensive cloud spirals and bands near and to the east of the closed low/troughs aloft. These also help estimate of the location of the bad weather area associated with the upper level disturbances.

   b. Compare your three estimates of the location of the "bad weather area" associated with each trough: (1) the area between the trough and downstream ridge, (2) the 500 mb temperature-dewpoint spread, and (3) the cloud cover from the IR satellite image. How do the locations and

NAME: _____

DATE: _____ CLASS: _____

the sizes of these areas compare? If you had to choose one analysis
method to locate the bad weather areas with speed and accuracy, which
would you choose?

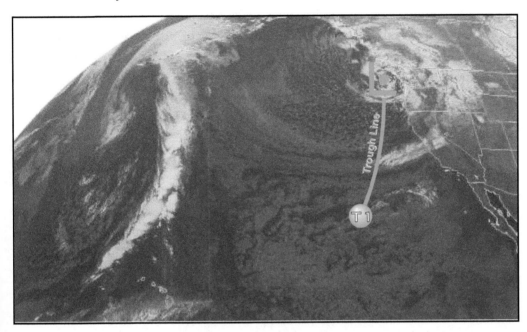

Figure 11-5. GOES West IR Satellite Image. 9 Oct 97

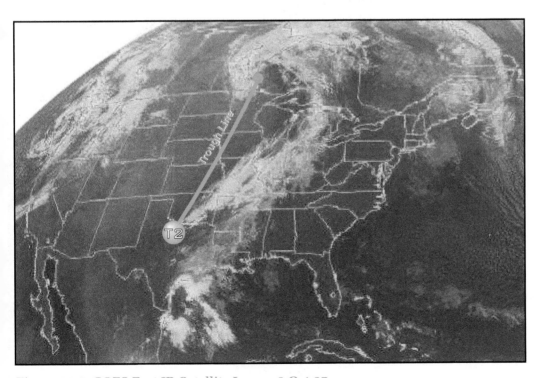

Figure 11-6. GOES East IR Satellite Image. 9 Oct 97

CAUTION: The areas of "bad weather" isolated in this task have been related to the extensive cloud cover caused by extratropical cyclones and associated frontal systems. Other "bad weather" areas may exist. Two examples are very windy cloud-free areas, and regions of low ceilings and visibility where low cloud tops are relatively warm and not obvious in IR imagery. Daytime visible imagery will aid in the location of the latter areas. METAR observations are always a useful supplement to satellite imagery.

TASK 11-4: LINKING THE SURFACE AND UPPER AIR STRUCTURE OF ET CYCLONES.

Figure 11-7 shows surface conditions for the same time as figure 11-3.

1. In general, where do you expect to find the location of a typical upper-level trough line relative to the center of a surface low-pressure system before the cyclone has occluded? (If you are not sure, consult figures 8-12 and 8-13 in *Aviation Weather.*)

2. In general, where do you expect to find the center of the closed low aloft relative to the center of the surface low-pressure system after the cyclone has occluded?

3. Consider the surface low-pressure area in western Ontario in figure 11-7.

   a. In what stage of development is the cyclone?

   b. The upper level disturbance (wave trough) is located to the (west of, east of, same location as) _____ the surface low.

4. Consider the surface cyclone on the West Coast of the U.S. in figure 11-7.

   a. In what stage of development is the cyclone?

   b. The upper level disturbance (closed low) is located (upstream of, downstream of, at the same location as) _____ the surface low.

NAME: _____

DATE: _____ CLASS: _____

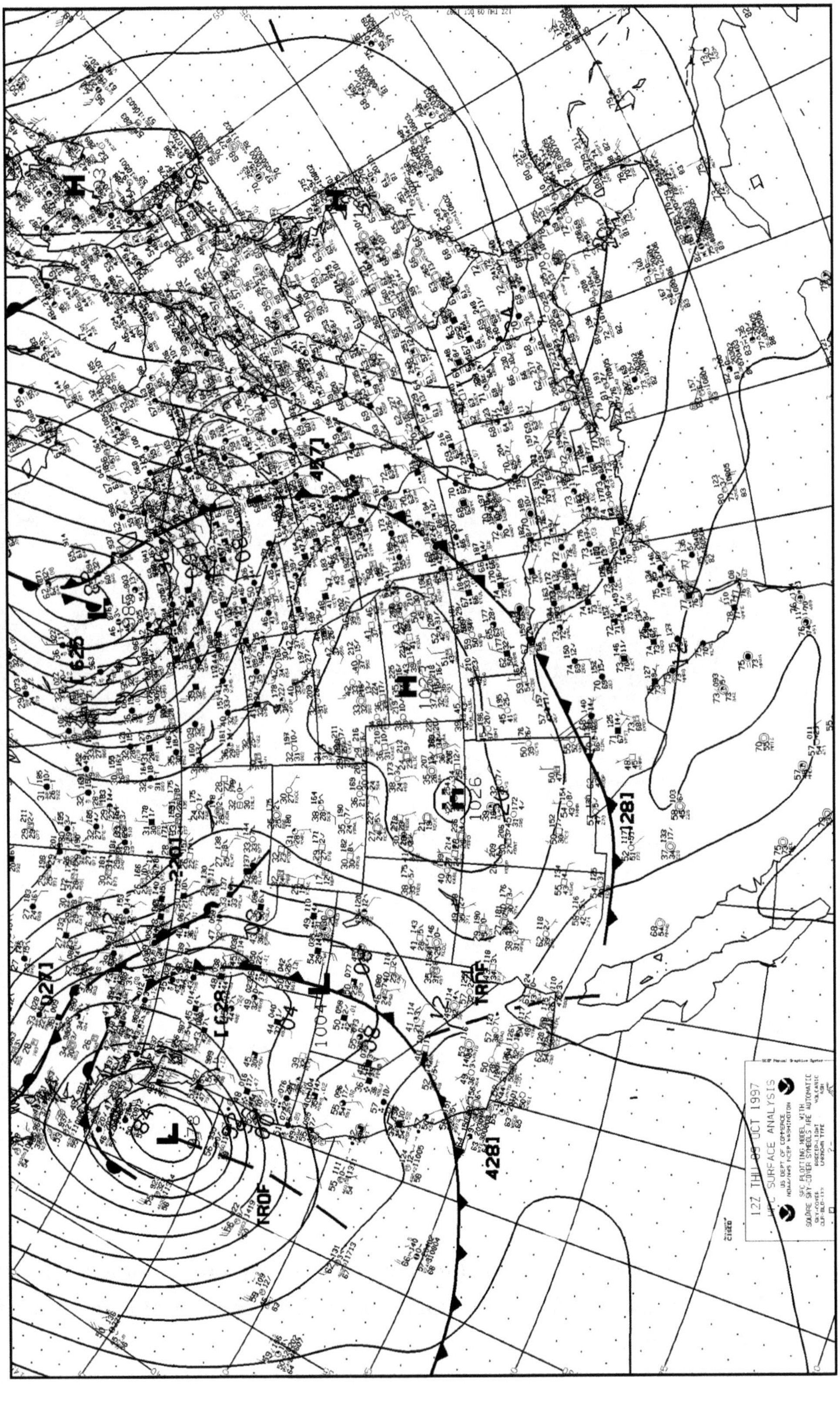

Figure 11-7. Surface Analysis Chart for 9 October 97, 1200 UTC.

5. Inspect the satellite images in figures 11-5 and 11-6 and note the location of each trough line relative to the major cloud features. Notice that the trough line is drawn from the center of the cloud hook (or spiral) to the end of the brightest band extending to the south of the disturbance. This configuration is illustrated in the schematic diagram in figure 11-8. Use this information to draw the trough line in the disturbance over the central Pacific in figure 11-5. Draw a single heavy line and label it "trough."

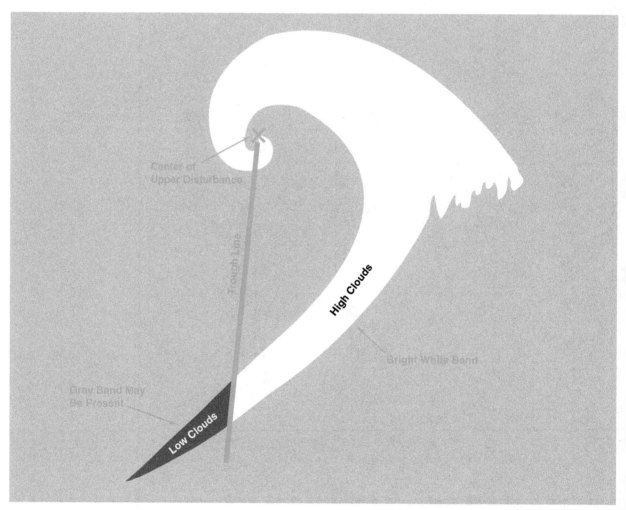

Figure 11-8. Diagram of the relation between the location of the upper level trough line and the satellite-view of the cloud features (infrared imagery).

CAUTION: Keep in mind that satellite images are a "top down" view of cloud layers. High level clouds often hide important low-level features of ET cyclones, such as warm fronts.

NAME: _____

DATE: _____ CLASS: _____

QUESTIONS

1. On a constant pressure analysis chart, the location of a station can be plotted with a circle, star, or rectangle. What do these symbols mean?

2. The 700 mb chart has many of the characteristics of the 500 mb chart; however, there are some differences. For example, the 700 mb chart is at a lower level in the troposphere. What is the standard height of 700 mb? Are there any places on the globe where surface friction influences winds at 700 mb?

3. Use an ordinary pencil to draw two diagrams of an extratropical cyclone with fronts and isobars, as they would appear on a surface weather analysis chart. In the first diagram, show the early (incipient wave) stage. In the second diagram, show the same cyclone 24 hours later in the fully occluded stage. Be sure to use the proper symbols for each type of front. In a different color, superimpose the 500 mb contours of a wave cyclone over each diagram.

EXERCISE 12:

JET STREAMS

OBJECTIVES:

- To introduce you to the jet stream charts (300 mb, 250 mb, 200 mb), and their analysis and interpretation
- To become familiar with the structure and features of jet streams

References: *Aviation Weather*, Chapter 7, "Scales of Atmospheric Circulation"; Chapter 8, "Airmasses, Fronts, and Cyclones"; Chapter 11, "Wind Shear"; Chapter 12, "Turbulence"; and Appendix D, "Standard Meteorological Codes and Graphics for Aviation." Supplemental reading: *AC 00-45F, Aviation Weather Services*, Sections 4.

BACKGROUND

A jet stream is a narrow band of high speed winds (usually exceeding 60 knots) found near the tropopause. The polar front jet stream occurs mainly in midlatitudes in the vicinity of the polar front. It is stronger in the winter and weaker in the summer. The subtropical jet stream is found around 25° to 30° of latitude and only exists during the cooler part of the year. Jet streams reach their greatest speeds at the tropopause. For this reason, constant pressure charts near the tropopause (300 mb, 250 mb, 200 mb) show wind speed analyses as well as contours and isotherms. Figure 12-1 shows examples of polar front and subtropical jet streams on a 250 mb constant pressure chart. The jet stream axis is the line of maximum winds on the chart. The axis is not usually shown on these charts; rather, it is implied from the wind speed analysis. In figure 12-1, the jet axis has been added for clarity. Also see figure 7-9 in *Aviation Weather*.

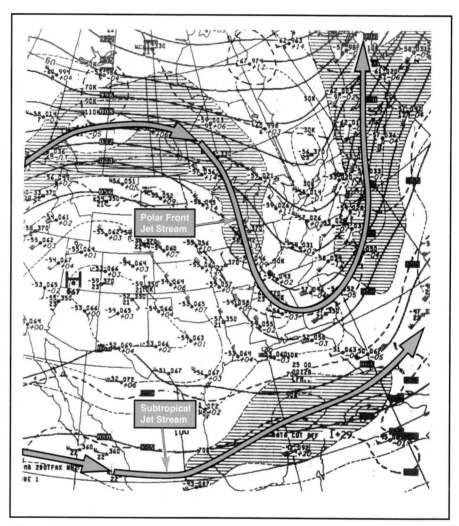

Figure 12-1. 250 mb Constant Pressure Chart. Jet stream axes are indicated by thick lines with arrowheads.

As you know from *Aviation Weather* and Exercise 1, the **tropopause** has an average altitude of about 36,000 feet; however, it is significantly higher over warm tropical regions and lower over cold polar regions. Furthermore, the tropopause is lower over cold ET cyclones and troughs aloft and higher over warm highs and ridges aloft. Near jet streams, the tropopause altitude changes rapidly from the polar side of the jet (low tropopause) to the equatorial side (high tropopause). These features are illustrated in figure 7-10 in *Aviation Weather*.

In this exercise, you will examine the horizontal structure of jet streams. You also will become familiar with jet stream charts.

NAME: _____

DATE: _____ CLASS: _____

TASK 12-1: JET STREAM CHART FAMILIARIZATION.

Figure 12-2 is a 300 mb constant pressure chart. This is one of three, so-called jet stream charts. The others are the 250 mb and 200 mb constant pressure analyses. They are called "jet stream charts" because the jet stream is a common feature of the wind field at those levels. When you compare jet stream charts with 850 mb, 700 mb, or 500 mb charts, it is obvious that there is more information on the higher level charts. In addition to contours and isotherms, isotachs (lines of constant speed) are also shown.

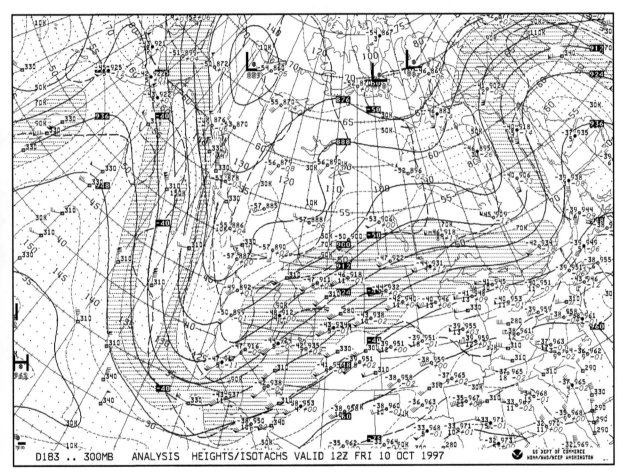

D183 .. 300MB   ANALYSIS   HEIGHTS/ISOTACHS VALID 12Z FRI 10 OCT 1997

US DEPT OF COMMERCE
NOAA/NWS/NCEP WASHINGTON

Figure 12-2. 300 mb Constant Pressure Chart, 10 OCT 97 12Z.

1. First, review the chart to familiarize yourself with the new information. Identify the contours (solid), isotherms (thick dashed), and isotachs (thin dashed). Clearly label one of each of these lines over central Canada.

2. What is the meaning of the shaded portions of the map?

3. Use a red pencil to lightly trace each isotach on figure 12-2. Trace only those isotachs with speeds of **70 knots or greater**.

4. The isotachs are drawn at _____ knot intervals.

5. Shade the isotach analysis in red where winds exceed 110 knots.

6. The highest **reported** wind speed on the map is _____ knots.

7. The wind direction and wind speed at 36N and 131W is _____° at _____ knots.

NAME: _____

DATE: _____ CLASS: _____

TASK 12-2: THE JET AXIS.

Notice in figures 12-1 and 12-2 that the isotachs are stretched out in the direction of the wind. This elongated pattern is typical of jet streams. Jet streams are typically 1,000 nautical miles or more long and a few hundred nautical miles wide. Recall that the jet stream axis is a line of maximum winds on a jet stream chart. It is useful to know the location of the jet axis because temperature, wind, turbulence, and other weather conditions change rapidly across the axis. Although the jet stream axis is not shown on most jet stream charts, its position is easily implied from the isotach patterns. In contrast, the jet axis is shown on high level significant weather prognostic charts, but isotachs are not. You must be familiar with the relation between the jet axis and the wind speed pattern in order to interpret either chart.

Examine figure 12-1 to see how the jet axis is placed according to the isotach pattern. If the jet stream is strong, well defined, and the axis properly located, then a simple rule applies: as you move away from the jet axis, the wind speed always decreases.

1. Use the jet axis definition and the rule given above to estimate the position of all jet axes in figure 12-2. Draw each axis as a thick black line with arrowheads to indicate its direction. **Do not draw axes for winds below 70 knots.**

2. Although the wind speed variation is greater across than along any jet stream, wind speeds do vary along the jet axis. Elongated regions of strong winds embedded in the general jet stream structure are called jet streaks. For example, a jet streak with maximum winds exceeding 90 knots corresponds with the shaded region over the Gulf of Mexico along the subtropical jet stream axis in figure 12-1. These maximum wind regions move with the jet stream, but at a significantly slower rate than the jet stream winds. Jet streaks are important because they are often connected with the development of an ET cyclone. Locate and label the strongest jet streak in figure 12-2.

QUESTIONS

The shortest distance between two points on the earth is a great circle route, but the great circle route is not necessarily the fastest route, especially in the vicinity of the jet stream. The fastest route is called the "minimum time track (MTT)." You are flying a B747 between A and B at a typical cruise altitude for that aircraft. (See Figure 12-3.) The map is valid for the time of the flight. The map has been constructed so that the straight line between points A and B is a great circle route. The distance between those two points is 1,000 nautical miles. Jet stream information in the form of the 250 mb isotach pattern has been superimposed on the map. The location of the center of a cyclone is indicated by the "L." Use this information and your knowledge of jet streams to answer the following questions.

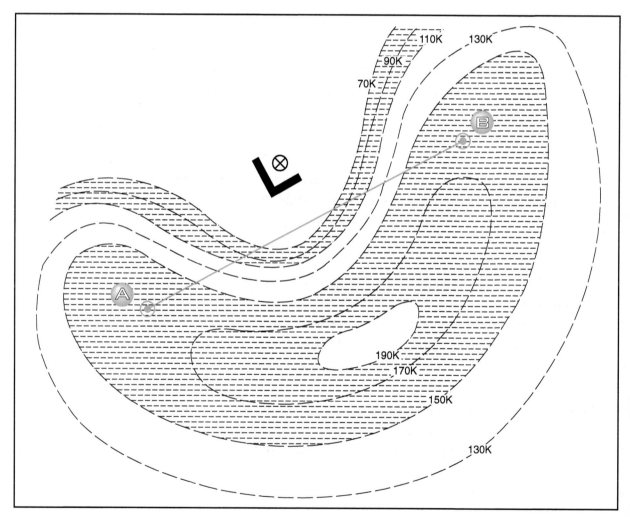

Figure 12-3. 250 mb Chart.

NAME: _____

DATE: _____   CLASS: _____

1. The standard altitude of a 250 mb chart is _____ .

2. Inspect the map carefully and estimate the MTT for a flight from A to B. There are techniques to do this very accurately, but for the purposes of this question, a reasonable "eyeball" estimate of the MTT is acceptable. Draw the MTT on the chart with a solid red line.

3. Use dashed red to show the estimated MTT on the return flight (B to A).

4. How would the MTTs you estimated in questions 2 and 3 change if you were flying a supersonic aircraft at Mach 2 at 63,000 feet rather than the B747? Why? Indicate your MTT estimates for the higher-flying aircraft in blue. (Hint: In addition to typical supersonic speeds, consider the flight altitude and the vertical extent of the jet stream.)

EXERCISE 13:

PILOT WEATHER REPORTS (PIREPs)

OBJECTIVES:

- To practice decoding, encoding, and interpreting PIREPs

References: *Aviation Weather*, Chapter 11, "Wind Shear" (page 11-10) and Appendix D, "Standard Meteorological Codes and Graphics for Aviation." Supplemental reading: *AC 00-45F, Aviation Weather Services*, Section 2.

BACKGROUND DISCUSSION

Pilot weather reports (PIREPs) provide you with valuable information about the nature of the weather from a pilot's point of view. They often confirm such information as the height of cloud bases, tops of cloud layers, in-flight visibility, icing conditions, wind direction, wind speed, turbulence, and other weather hazards. When significant aviation weather conditions are reported or forecast, air traffic control facilities are required to solicit PIREPs. You are encouraged to make a pilot report anytime you encounter unexpected weather condition. Your PIREPs benefit other pilots, aviation weather forecasters, and controllers. In this exercise you will decode and encode PIREPs and then interpret some actual reports.

TASK 13-1: PIREP DECODING.

A list of coded PIREPs is given in table 13-1. Decode the PIREPs and complete table 13-2.

```
                        TABLE 13-1
                     CODED PIREPs

 1.  DEC UA /OV DNV/TM 0030/FL070/TP C206/SK SCT 030 CA/TA 6C TB LGT
         CHOP/RM OVR DNV IN CLR AT 070 SCT CLDS BLO CLR ABV LTGIC DSTN S-W =

 2.  ORD UUA /OV ORD-RBS/TM 0249/FL310/TP B767/SK OVC 300 CA/TB LGT-MDT
         135-300/IC NEG/RM COUPLE OF SVR JOLTS GOING THRU 270 DURGC SWBND =

 3.  MDW UA /OV MDW120045/TM 0808/FL050/TP C206/SK OVC 045/TA 35F/TB
         LGT/IC NEG =

 4.  MDW UA /OV EON/TM 1208/FL090/TP C421/SK OVC 048 CA/IC LGT RIME/RM
         MOST OF THE ICE WAS NEAR THE TOPS =

 5.  BFL UA /OV SAC-BFL/TM 2104/FL090/TP C414/RM OTP 070 THROUGH-OUT
         TIL CZQ OCNL MOD TURBC IN CLDS DURGC/DURGD =

 6.  PRB UUA /OV AVE 080020/TM 1955/FL160/TP E2/IC MDT-SVR RIME/RM IN
         FREEZING RAIN/ZOA =

 7.  VNY UUA /OV FIM 148012/TM 0120/FL160/TP C500/TB HVY-MDT =


 8.  UIN UA /OV UIN 150018/TM 1211/FL030/TP BE18/IC TRACE MXD/RM
         FM ZKC =

 9.  CMI UA /OV CMI/TM 1326/FL020/TP E110/SK BKN V OVC 065/TB SMTH 070-020
         /R BLO 020 =

10.  RFD UA /OV RFD/TM 1329/FLDURC/TP C421/SK 28 AGL OVC 055 MSL CA/TA -8C
         FL120/TB SMOOTH/IC NONE =

11.  ORD UA /OV EON/TM 1429/FLDURC/TP PA31/SK OVC 042 070 OVC 075 CA/TA
         -5C FL090/IC TRACE IC LWR LYR =
```

NAME: _____

DATE: _____ CLASS: _____

TABLE 13-2
DECODED PIREPS

Location	Time (UTC)	Altitude (FT)	Acft. Type	Sky Cover Visibility/Weather	Temp (°C)	Turbulence	Icing	Remarks
1. DEC								
2. ORD								
3. MDW								
4. MDW								
5. BFL								
6. PRB								
7. VNY								
8. UIN								
9. CMI								
10. RFD								
11. ORD								

TASK 13-2: PIREP ENCODING.

The two situations described below must be reported as PIREPs. Encode them in the spaces provided.

1. You are flying a Piper Seneca, PA34, at 10,000 feet MSL. It is 0821 MST. You are over Laramie, Wyoming. As you were climbing out a few minutes ago, you passed through a layer of scattered clouds with bases at 8,000 feet MSL and tops at 9,000 feet MSL. There was no turbulence.

   Coded:

2. It is 11:37 pm EST over Tampa, Florida. You are flying a B747 at 39,000 feet. The measured wind velocity is west at 20 knots. The outside air temperature is −39°C. You are experiencing occasional moderate turbulence.

   Coded:

TASK 13-3: PIREP INTERPRETATION.

1. Three PIREPs are given below. Figure 13-1 is a cross section along the 070° radial from QQQ. Draw a schematic of the reported sky conditions based on the three PIREPs. QQQ is at sea level. Label the schematic clearly, indicating any apparent changes in the sky condition with distance from QQQ.

UA/OV QQQ070025/TM 1659/DURC/TP B737/SK 025 BKN 060

UA/OV QQQ/TM 1715/FL065/TP C172/SK OVC 055/TA 04

UA/OV QQQ070045/TM 1725/FL020/TP MO20/SK 025 SCT/TA 08

NAME: _____

DATE: _____ CLASS: _____

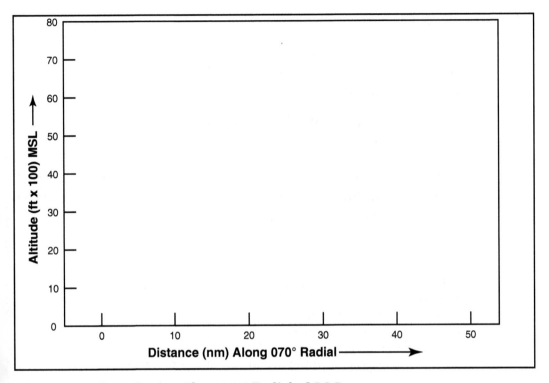

Figure 13-1. Cross Section Along 070° Radial of QQQ.

2. How would the flight conditions be different if QQQ in the previous question was actually Dallas, Texas?

3. What do you deduce about the flight conditions over ABC from the following PIREPs?

```
UA/OV ABC/TM 0800/FL090/TP UNKN/RM CLR

UA/OV ABC/TM 1002/DURD/TP BE02/SK 025 SCT 060/TA -5/RM TB
     SMTH

UA/OV ABC/TM 1222/FL030 /TP PA28/SK IMC/ WX FV01 R
```

QUESTIONS

1. When a radial and distance from a navigation aid is used to identify the location of a PIREP, is the direction magnetic or true? _____ Is the distance statute or nautical miles? _____

2. Are the wind directions given in a PIREP magnetic or true? _____ What units are used for the wind speeds? _____

3. Another type of PIREP is called an AIREP (ARP). It is a meteorological report made at predetermined intervals by commercial airliners. The information reported includes:

   Flight number
   Position (latitude/longitude in degrees and usually hundredths)
   Time (UTC)
   Flight level (F) in hundreds of feet
   Temperature in °C (MS means minus)
   Wind direction (°) and wind speed (knots)
   Occasional remarks regarding turbulence (TB) and weather (WX)

Give the plain language interpretation for the following AIREPs.

```
ARP KLM601 6300N 3000W 1535 F330 MS50 180/045KT=



ARP UAL2 4100N 1400W 1529 F370 MS53 217/147KT=



ARP AAL515 2330N 6743W 2302 F350 MS45 150/003KT TB SMOOTH=



ARP TWA903 42N 050W F390 MS55 265/50KT TB LGT CHOP WX 42N45W
    MS56 285/035 TB NIL=
```

NOTE: In the last few years, the number of reports has grown rapidly with the addition of automated Aircraft Meteorological Data Relay (AMDAR) systems.

EXERCISE 14:

THUNDERSTORMS

OBJECTIVES:
- To become familiar with the radar summary chart and the lifted index chart
- To understand the relation of large-scale weather patterns to thunderstorm development
- To review the properties of thunderstorms as revealed by direct observations

References: *Aviation Weather*, Chapter 9, "Thunderstorms"; Chapter 11, "Wind Shear"; Chapter 12, "Turbulence"; and Appendix D, "Meteorological Codes and Graphics for Aviation." Supplemental reading: *AC 00-45F, Aviation Weather Services*, Sections 3 and 4.

BACKGROUND DISCUSSION

Thunderstorms can produce some of the worst aviation weather hazards. Minimizing the impact of thunderstorms requires the ability to identify them, evaluate their intensity, and track their movement. In this exercise, you will see how weather products are used to diagnose thunderstorm activity. You will see what causes thunderstorms and what their effects are. The tasks in this exercise provide you with practice interpreting the information on radar summary charts and recognizing areas of potential thunderstorm activity on large-scale weather charts. It also includes a comparison of large-scale thunderstorm indicators with actual thunderstorm observations from weather radar and satellites. The exercise concludes with the examination of thunderstorm effects as documented in METARs and PIREPs. A thorough review of the references listed above is required before attempting this exercise.

TASK 14-1: RADAR SUMMARY CHART FAMILIARIZATION.

There are two very useful weather charts that give you a "quick look" at weather conditions with emphasis on the most common aviation weather hazards. One is the weather depiction chart, which graphically displays areas of IFR, MVFR, and VFR conditions. The use of this chart is covered in Exercise 15. The second chart is the radar summary chart. It is a graphical presentation of weather radar reports from weather radar sites across the country. It gives you a quick look at areas of precipitation and is especially useful for identifying thunderstorms and assessing their intensity. A typical radar summary chart is shown in figure 14-1.

1. Radar echoes in figure 14-1 are delineated by one or more contours. How do the contours relate to the intensity of the echoes?

2. Highlight in red the areas on figure 14-1 with radar echo intensity levels greater than three. What is the significance of intensity level to the pilot?

3. List the maximum and minimum height of echo tops reported on figure 14-1. Circle the location of these extremes and label them clearly.

    Maximum _____ feet

    Minimum _____ feet

NAME: _____

DATE: _____ CLASS: _____

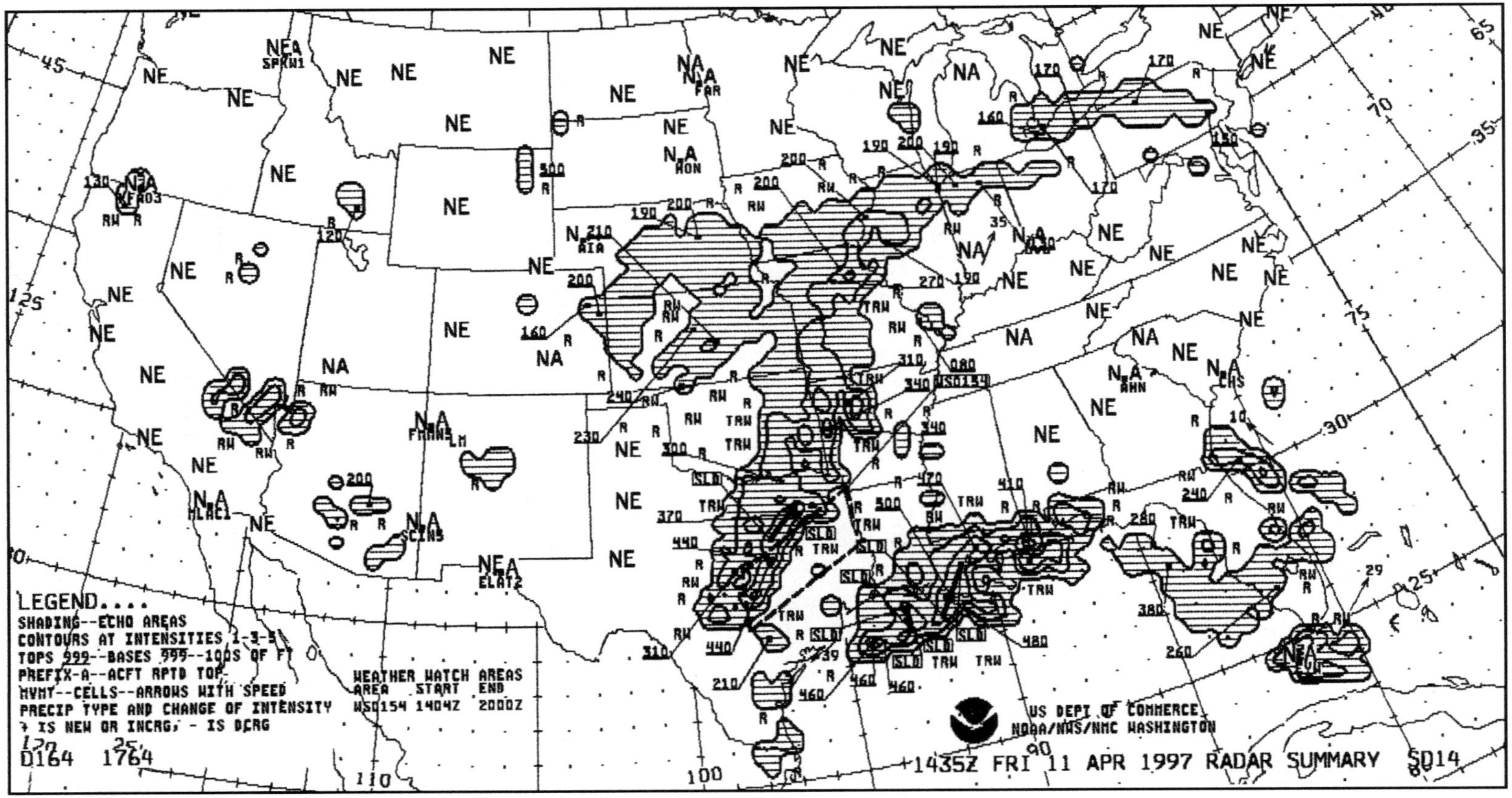

Figure 14-1. Radar Summary Chart.

CAUTION: Individual radar echoes typically move, grow, die, and regenerate over periods of an hour or less. Although they are very useful, radar summary charts are only crude snapshots of this process and may be more than an hour old when you see them.

4. Are the heights of echoes (bases and tops) MSL or AGL?

5. What do the following abbreviations mean?

R

RW

TRW

SLD

6. In the state of Indiana, there is an arrow with the number "35" near the arrowhead. Explain this symbol.

7. A dashed line encloses a box in eastern Texas in figure 14-1. What does this box represent? When is it valid?

TASK 14-2: THUNDERSTORMS AND LARGE-SCALE WEATHER CONDITIONS.

The purpose of this task is to help you understand the connection between thunderstorms observed by radar and satellite, and the large-scale weather patterns that you see on surface weather analysis charts and constant pressure charts. As a starting point, be sure to review *Aviation Weather*, Chapter 9, Section E under

NAME: _____

DATE: _____ CLASS: _____

the heading "Instability Patterns" and Appendix D, page D-20 on the "Lifted Index Analysis Chart."

As you have learned from your text, there are two requirements for thunderstorms:
- **initial lift**, and
- **large instability**.

1. Initial lift refers to the lifting of the air by some circulation or circulation feature to set off the instability. After the instability is released, free convection takes over and the buoyant air rises on its own.

   Examine the surface analysis and 500 mb constant pressure charts in figures 14-2 and 14-3. They are valid for the same date and time. Identify those circulation features that can cause lifting. Use an ordinary pencil to neatly enclose each suspected area. In a convenient space next to each area, write the type of lifting you have identified, such as "frontal lifting."

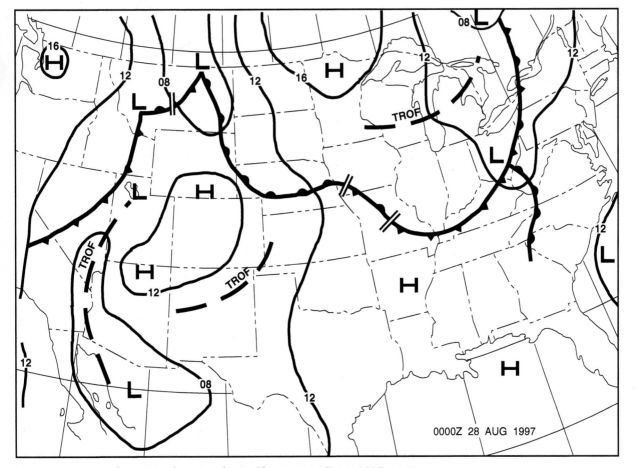

Figure 14-2. Surface Weather Analysis Chart, 0000Z 28 AUG 1997.

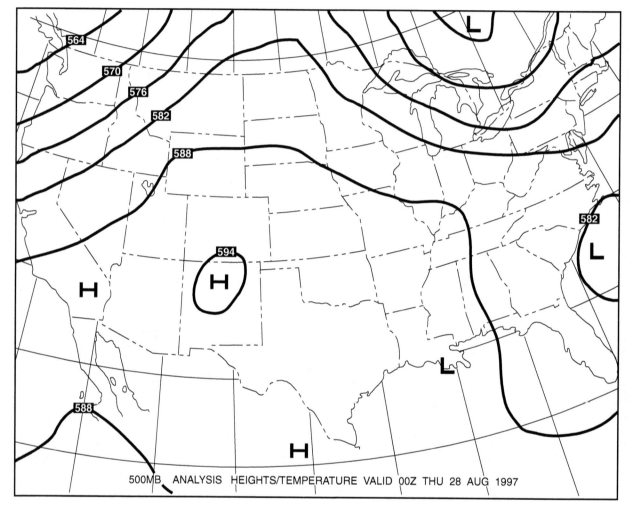

500MB ANALYSIS HEIGHTS/TEMPERATURE VALID 00Z THU 28 AUG 1997

Figure 14-3. 500 mb Constant Pressure Chart, 0000Z 28 AUG 1997.

2. Large instability. As you can see from the previous task, there are many regions where air may be rising. Clouds and precipitation will be found in those areas where there is adequate moisture and lifting, but thunderstorms will only occur if the air has large instability. In order to evaluate the situation, meteorologists examine the details of things such as surface heating, cooling aloft, the vertical distribution of temperature and moisture, and low-level moisture convergence. Although many of these analyses are beyond the scope of this course, you can use your knowledge of **stability indexes** as a preliminary measure of the degree of instability.

An example of a lifted index analysis chart from a "composite moisture chart" is presented in figure 14-4. The chart is valid for the same date and time as the charts in figures 14-2 and 14-3. Use this chart to answer the following questions.

NAME: _____

DATE: _____ CLASS: _____

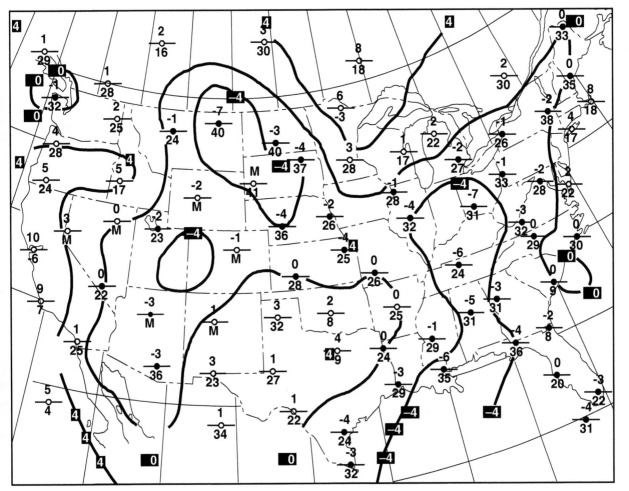

Figure 14-4. Lifted Index Analysis Chart, 0000Z 28 AUG 1997.

a. How many times a day is this panel available? What are the contours on the chart?

b. Explain Lifted Index. Place a red circle around the LI at Miami.

    c.   What are the units of LI?

    d.   Define the K Index. Place a red circle around the K Index at San Diego.

    e.   To evaluate the instability pattern, use an ordinary pencil and draw lines on the stability panel to enclose the area or areas where the probability of an airmass thunderstorm exceeds 50%. (Hint: use the K index.)

    f.   In light red, shade the areas where LI is less than zero; and in dark red, shade the areas where it is less than −4. Do not obliterate data. What is the significance of a Lifted Index of less than −4?

3. **Comparisons with Radar and Satellite Observations.** Now that you have identified the areas that are most likely associated with thunderstorms, you will compare them with actual observations of thunderstorms. Figure 14-5 is the radar summary chart for about the same time as figures 14-2, 14-3, and 14-4. Figure 14-6 is the corresponding infrared satellite image from GOES 8. From Exercise 9, recall that the IR image provides temperature information from clouds and surface features.

NAME: _____

DATE: _____ CLASS: _____

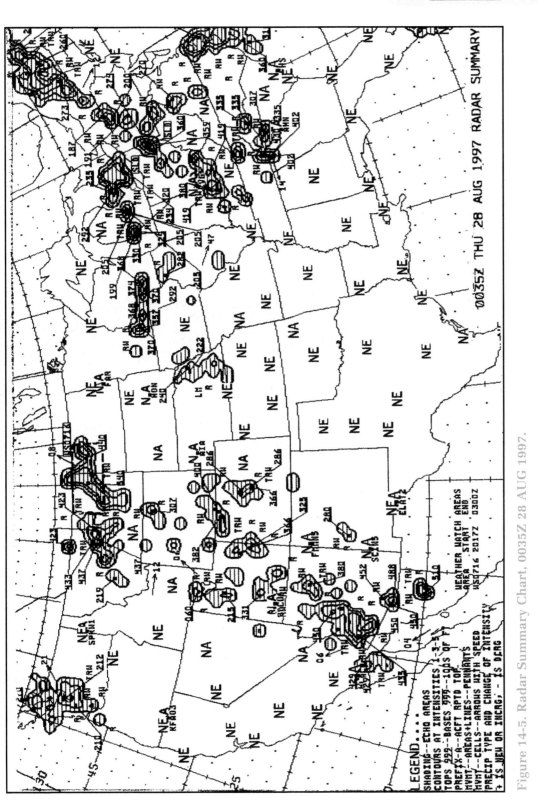

Figure 14-5. Radar Summary Chart, 0035Z 28 AUG 1997.

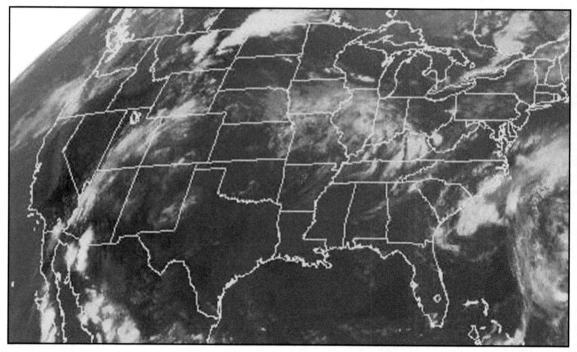

Figure 14-6. GOES 8 IR Image, 0015Z 28 AUG 1997.

a. It is important to know the local times across the country in order to
find out what role solar heating plays in the development of thunderstorms. The time of the radar summary chart, 0035Z, corresponds to
the following standard times:

EST _____

CST _____

MST_____

PST _____

b. What evidence tells you that the majority of the echoes in figure 14-5
are associated with thunderstorms?

NAME: _____

DATE: _____   CLASS: _____

c.   Compare the echo regions in figure 14-5 with the large-scale areas you identified as being subjected to **both** rising motion **and** large instability in task 14-2, questions 1 and 2. Prepare a brief discussion of the comparison. (Hint: the basic question is, are the thunderstorms where you expected them to be? Why?)

d.   In figure 14-5, use a red pencil to highlight echo tops in excess of 40,000 feet.

e.   On the satellite image in figure 14-6, draw a red line around the cloud features that correspond to the highest echo tops identified in the previous question.

f.   What do you conclude about the highest echo tops and the brightness of the cloud tops? Why does this relationship exist?

g.   On the radar summary chart in figure 14-5, notice the W-E line of radar echoes that stretches from southeastern Minnesota across southern Wisconsin. On figure 14-6, circle the cloud pattern on the satellite image that corresponds with this line of echoes. What feature do you find in this area on the surface analysis chart in figure 14-2? Why is a line of thunderstorms related to the particular surface feature?

h. According to all the information in figures 14-2 through 14-6, between 0000Z and 0035Z on August 28th, 1997, in what state were the most severe thunderstorms occurring? Why? List all your evidence.

i. On figure 14-3, the Lifted Index along the Gulf Coast is as low as −6 with a K index of 35 at the same location; yet, according the radar summary chart in figure14-5 and the IR satellite image in figure 14-6, there is no thunderstorm activity in that area. Give a reasonable explanation.

NAME: _____

DATE: _____ CLASS: _____

TASK 14-3: THUNDERSTORM EFFECTS.

In this final task of the exercise, your attention is turned to thunderstorm effects.

1. **METAR** reports are useful indicators of the presence of thunderstorms and their influence on the local airspace. Table 14-1 is a list of five METARs, each of which has important information regarding thunderstorms. For each METAR, give a plain language statement of the thunderstorm-related conditions. Note that "thunderstorm-related conditions" refer to any reported parameter or condition, or reported change in a parameter or condition related to the presence of a thunderstorm at, or near, the observing station.

TABLE 14-1. METAR REPORTS

KFHU 160157Z 28008KT 250V330 30SM FEW065CB SCT110 BKN250 26/17 A3015 RMK ONCL
 LTGIC CB DSNT SE-S=

KGBN 160155Z 03016G25KT 20SM TS SCT080CB SCT150 BKN250 35/18 A2985 RMK TS NE MOV
 NE SLP092 CB NE-E-SE MOV NE=

KIWA 160145Z 25008KT 20SM SCT060CB BKN200 34/17 A2989 RMK CB DSNT SE OCNL LTGCG
 DSNT SE=

KPHX 160156Z 32006KT 10SM FEW080CB SCT150 OVC250 34/19 A2985 RMK AO2 WSHFT 0047
 RAB00E13 SLP088 OCNL LTG DSNT NE P0001 T03390194=

KBRO 111334Z 35009G20KT 3/4SM +TSRA BR BKN002 BKN007 OVC010 21/20
 A2996 RMK AO2 PRESRR P0075=

Plain Language Interpretation of Thunderstorm-Related Conditions

KFHU

KGBN

KIWA

KPHX

KBRO

2. **PIREPs** also provide useful information with regard to thunderstorms. Table 14-2 is a list of five PIREPs that are associated with thunderstorm conditions. Give clear, plain language interpretations and explanations of the flight hazards and their thunderstorm-related causes based on the PIREPs. Sketches will help.

TABLE 14-2. THUNDERSTORM-RELATED PIREPs.

```
MIA UUA/OV MIA/TM 1915/FL ON FNL APRCH/TP MD80/RM LOSS OF 20
    KNOTS AT 300FT APPROACHING MIDDLE MARKER 27 RIGHT.
MOD UA /OV FAT-MCE-MOD/TM 0041/TP UNK/SK SCT-BKN 065-085/RM TCU BLDG
    OVR SIERRA/ DETERIORATING CONDITIONS
ICT UA /OV ICT/TM 2200/FL090/TP BE90/TB LGT-OCNL MDT/RM SMOOTH OUTSIDE
    LN OF TS
SGF UA /OV SGF/TM 2044/FL220/TP C130/WV 193110/RM PICKING WAY THRU TRW
    TOPS
YVR UUA/OV LANGLEY B.C./TM 2010/ FL ON GND/RM HAIL 3-4MM DIAMETER
```

MIA:

MOD:

NAME: _____

DATE: _____ CLASS: _____

ICT:

SGF:

YVR:

QUESTIONS

1. What is the difference between the cross-sectional area of a weather radar echo (e.g. on a PPI scope) and the actual cross-sectional area of the cloud that contains the echo?

2A. What do the contours on a radar summary chart represent?

2B. Echo intensity is specified on some charts as lines corresponding to certain dBZ values. What is 'dBZ'? How does it relate to the contour values on the Radar Summary Chart?

3. Besides echo intensity, what other information is provided by Doppler weather radar?

4. The following letters and numbers often appear on radar summary charts. What is their meaning?

NE

OM

TRW

WS880

WT250

S

5. The altitude of a thunderstorm cloud top can be estimated from the temperature of the cloud top as measured by satellite. Will that altitude correspond to the top of the radar echo from the same thunderstorm if they are both measured at the same time? Why?

The following questions are based on the "convective outlook chart."

6. What is a convective outlook chart?

7. What forecast period does a convective outlook chart cover?

8. Explain the use of the term "SLGT" on a convective outlook chart.

9. (True, False) Only severe thunderstorm activity is predicted on the convective outlook chart.

10. Define "severe thunderstorm."

EXERCISE 15:

IMC AND ICING

OBJECTIVES:

- To review the weather-related factors that produce instrument meteorological conditions and icing
- To use weather reports and charts to locate some elementary meteorological indicators of instrument meteorological conditions and icing

References: *Aviation Weather* Chapter 6, "Atmospheric Moisture"; Chapter 13, "Icing"; Chapter 14, "Instrument Meteorological Conditions"; and Appendix D, "Standard Meteorological Codes and Graphics for Aviation." Supplemental reading: *AC 00-45F, Aviation Weather Services,* Section 4.

BACKGROUND DISCUSSION

This exercise addresses two important aviation weather hazards: instrument meteorological conditions (IMC) and icing. To successfully complete this exercise, you should be thoroughly familiar with the references dealing with moisture, IMC, and icing. In this exercise you will use METAR observations and meteorological charts, such as the weather depiction and surface analysis charts, to deduce actual and potential IMC conditions. You also will interpret PIREPs and conventional meteorological charts to isolate potential icing regions.

TASK 15-1: IMC AND METAR.

1. Define the following terms quantitatively.

VFR:

MVFR:

IFR:

LIFR:

2. Each of the following METAR reports has evidence of the presence of IMC conditions. In table 15-1, list the decoded information from each METAR.

```
KLIT 100615Z 30007KT 5SM BR BKN005 BKN012 09/09 A2966=

KCLE 231254Z 27010G18KT 6SM HZ BKN015 OVC023 03/M01 RMK AO2 SLP170 T00281006=

KCMH 231451Z 28016KT 9SM FEW021 BKN038 03/M02 A3007 RMK AO2 SLP189 T00331017
  53014 $=

KCEC 241750Z 34007KT 1/2SM FG OVC002 14/13 A2979 RMK SLP08810150 20139=

KHLR 241735Z 34014KT 7SM BKN028 26/16 A3001 RMK SLP149 ESTMD SLP=
```

TABLE 15-1. METAR REPORTS DECODED DATA

	Ceiling	Visibility	VFR? MVFR? IFR? LIFR?	Temperature/ Dewpoint Spread	Weather
KLIT	_____	_____	_____	_____	_____
KCLE	_____	_____	_____	_____	_____
KCMH	_____	_____	_____	_____	_____
KCEC	_____	_____	_____	_____	_____
KHLR	_____	_____	_____	_____	_____

NAME: _____

DATE: _____ CLASS: _____

TASK 15-2: IMC AND THE WEATHER DEPICTION CHART.

When you are planning a flight, one of the primary weather questions that you want to answer is, "Are there any problems?" The weather depiction chart is a useful "quick-look chart" for answering part of that question. It is a graphical presentation of weather, ceiling, and visibility information that is available from METARs. At a glance, you can see where IFR and MVR conditions existed at the time of the map, as well as weather phenomena that were causing them. An example is shown in figure 15-1. If you have read the material listed in the references of this exercise, then the legend on the map will serve as a meaningful review. This task gives you practice in the interpretation of the information on the weather depiction chart.

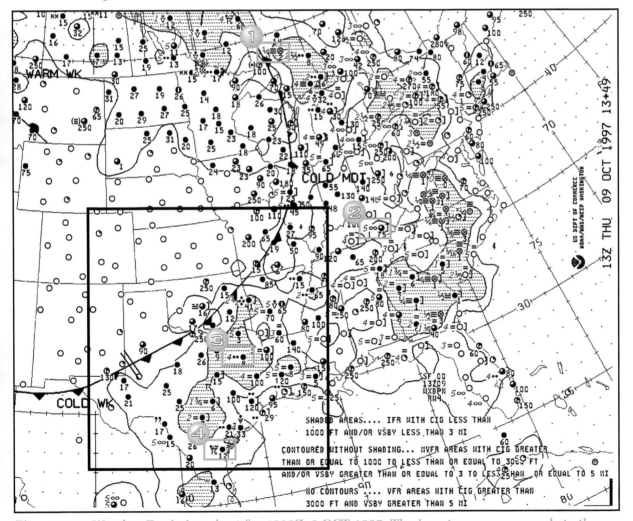

Figure 15-1. Weather Depiction chart for 1300Z, 9 OCT 1997. The insert area corresponds to the area in figure 15-2.

1. Identify the IFR regions in figure 15-1 by shading them lightly in red. Do not obliterate data.

2. Explain **ALL** of the symbols within the boxes numbered (1) through (4). In the space below, sketch each symbol, then give a brief, plain-language definition of the symbol. Be sure to include the symbol within the station circle.

(1)

(2)

(3)

(4)

NAME: _____

DATE: _____ CLASS: _____

3. A portion of a surface weather analysis chart is presented in figure 15-2. It was constructed an hour earlier than the weather depiction chart in figure 15-1. On figure 15-2, outline in green the areas where the surface temperature-dewpoint spread is 5F° or less. Outline and shade in red the areas where the spread is 2F° or less.

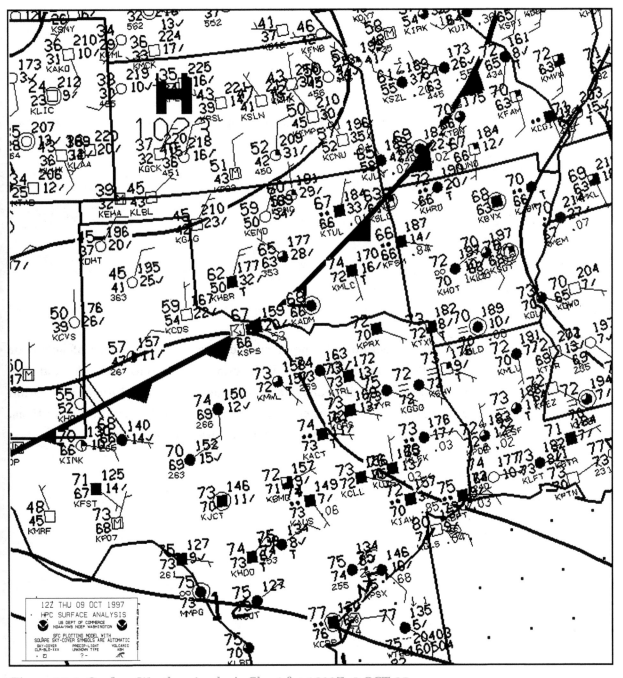

Figure 15-2. Surface Weather Analysis Chart for 1200Z, 9 OCT 97.

4. Compare your outlined and shaded regions on the surface weather analysis to the MVFR/IFR areas on the weather depiction chart in figure 15-1. What do you conclude?

5. State the rules of thumb that relate temperature-dewpoint spread to the presence of clouds or fog. (See Chapter 14 in *Aviation Weather.*) State rules in **both** °F and °C.

CAUTION: Temperature-dewpoint spread is a useful indicator of actual or potential IMC conditions when high humidity produces clouds and fog. However, IMC due to dry particulates, such as smoke, have little or no relation to the temperature-dewpoint spread. In fact, in forest fire weather conditions, the humidity is typically quite low and the spread large.

NAME: _____

DATE: _____ CLASS: _____

TASK 15-3: ICING AND PIREPS.

In this task, you will practice decoding PIREPs that document the presence of icing. Pay particular attention to the presence of "visible moisture," the air temperature, and icing remarks.

A series of PIREPs are given below. In table 15-2, write a **plain language** statement for each PIREP.

```
STC UA/OV STC 180075/TM 1356/FL 140/TP BE90/WX IMC/TA -10/WV
    255022/TB SMTH/IC NEG=

YYC UA/OV YYC 180020/TM 1446/FL 100-080/TP A32/IC CLR/RM
    ACCUMULATED 1/4 INCH CLR ICG=

PIH UA/OV PIH 180020/TM 1426/FL 110/TP PA31/IC LGT MXD=

RNO UA/OV RNO/TM 1434/FL 140/TP PA 31/SK OVC 110/IC LGT RIME=

RFD UA /OV RFD 180045/TM 0552/FL 080/TP C206/SK OTP/TA +2C/RM 25S RFD
    AT 080 IC TA -2C LGT-MDT ICE AT 060 TA +2C ON APCH BLO 040 LGT-MDT
    ICE=
```

TABLE 15-2. DECODED PIREPS

	Location	Altitude (ft MSL)	Sky Cover, Visibility Weather	OAT (°C)	Icing Conditions
STC	_____	_____	_____	_____	_____
YYC	_____	_____	_____	_____	_____
PIH	_____	_____	_____	_____	_____
RNO	_____	_____	_____	_____	_____
RFD	_____	_____	_____	_____	_____
	_____	_____	_____	_____	_____
	_____	_____	_____	_____	_____
	_____	_____	_____	_____	_____

TASK 15-4: ICING AND WEATHER PATTERNS.

You can estimate the potential for icing in a given weather situation by examining the temperature, cloud, and moisture patterns on conventional weather maps. In this task, you will apply your knowledge of icing processes and indicators to determine the possibility of structural icing below approximately 10,000 feet MSL. The primary tools for this task are the 850 mb and 700 mb constant pressure charts shown in figures 15-3 and 15-4.

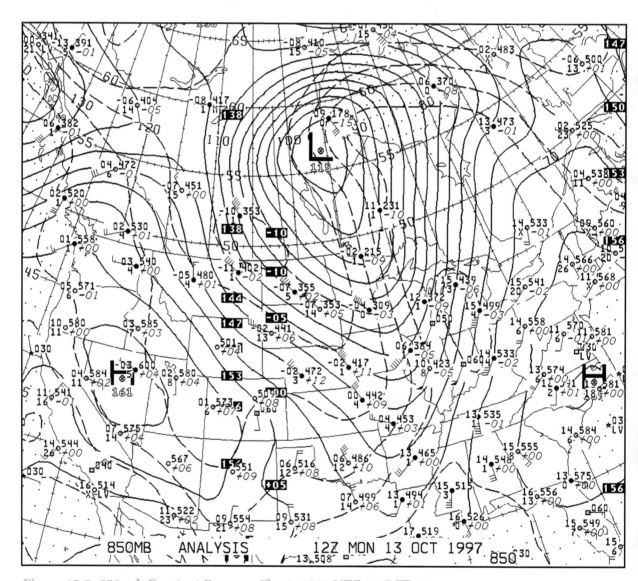

Figure 15-3. 850 mb Constant Pressure Chart, 1200 UTC 13 OCT 97.

NAME: _____

DATE: _____ CLASS: _____

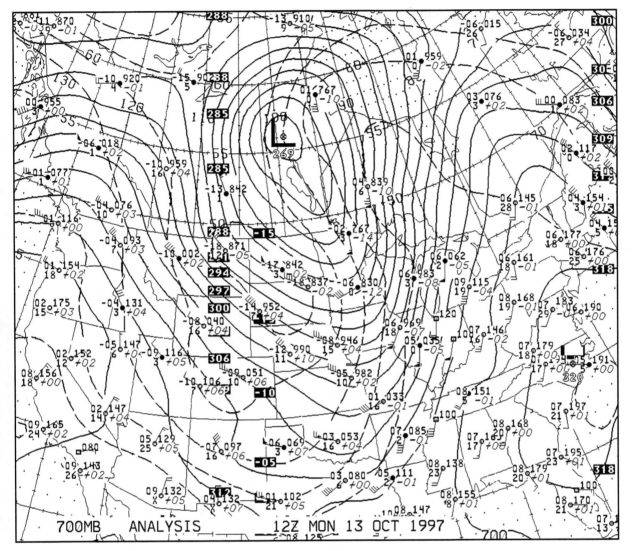

Figure 15-4. 700 mb Constant Pressure Chart, 1200 UTC 13 OCT 97.

1. What are the standard heights (in feet) of the 850 mb and 700 mb charts.
   850 mb = _____ feet
   700 mb = _____ feet

2. Use the 850 mb and 700 mb charts to identify regions with temperatures in the 0°C to −15°C range. In red pencil, carefully trace over the four critical isotherms in this range on each chart.

3. What is the significance of the 0°C to –15°C temperature range?

4. On each constant pressure chart, outline in green the area(s) where cloud layers are likely to exist. Use a critical temperature-dewpoint spread of 5C° or less. Do not obliterate data.

5. On each constant pressure chart, use a thick black pencil line to neatly enclose those regions where the temperature range is 0°C to –15°C **AND** the spread is 5C° or less. This is the suspected region of significant icing.

6. In red letters, label the interior of the icing regions as "CLEAR ICE" or "MIXED ICE" in the appropriate temperature ranges.

7. The probability that a solid cloud layer actually exists increases as the spread decreases. For example, if the temperature-dewpoint spread is 2C°, it is very likely that an overcast layer is present. How does your estimate of the icing area(s) change if the 2C° spread is used as the threshold for clouds rather than the 5C° threshold?

8. Are there any locations where the "visible moisture/critical temperature" method used here might have missed? Consider the surface weather analysis chart in figure 15-5 and the local terrain.

NAME: _____

DATE: _____ CLASS: _____

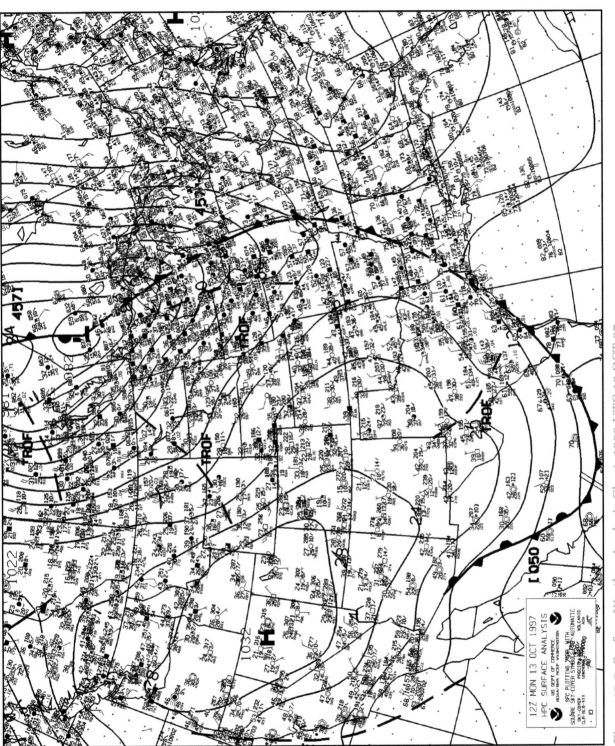

Figure 15-5. Surface Weather Analysis Chart, 1200 UTC 13 OCT 97.

CAUTIONS: If you have completed Task 15-3 successfully, your knowledge of where and how to look for evidence of icing has been substantially increased. Keep in mind that the icing estimate made here is very crude. It is based on relatively few observations at two horizontal levels separated by nearly 10,000 feet. Also, the presence of individual thunderstorm cells has not been considered. Furthermore, this estimate is not a prognosis — it is only a diagnosis. While the simple procedure used in this task is useful for instructional purposes and preliminary flight planning, more useful tools are available from NWS (e.g., AWC/ADDS ... see Question 8). Furthermore, this exercise, or any procedure dealing strictly with observed conditions, is NOT A FORECAST. Official NWS icing forecasts should be used for flight planning. Always get a legal brief.

QUESTIONS

1. What cautions should you be aware of when you use the weather depiction chart for flight planning?

2. Describe a situation where the ceiling and/or visibility defines MVFR or IFR conditions, yet the temperature-dewpoint spread is very large. (Use an example other than the one given in the "caution" at the end of Task 15-2.)

3. Two large-scale conditions that can lead to extensive IFR and MVFR conditions and, in winter, have serious icing potential are "overrunning" and "upslope" situations. Draw diagrams that illustrate the large-scale weather patterns for these conditions, as they would appear on a surface weather analysis chart.

4. In addition to reports of icing, what other useful information about icing can be obtained from PIREPs?

5. How can a weather radar chart be used to evaluate icing potential?

6. The difference in temperature between the 850 mb and 500 mb levels at a particular station can be used as an index for icing severity. Explain.

7. The advice for getting out of an icing situation in stratiform clouds is to either climb or descend (depending on altitude, terrain, and aircraft performance). Why is this action reasonable? Why is this advice less likely to be successful with icing in cumuliform clouds?

8. Current Icing Potential (CIP) and Forecast Icing Potential (FIP) charts are available from ADDS at http://adds.aviationweather.gov/icing/. Access that website and familiarize yourself with those products. Also examine the current and forecast freezing level charts. Finally, obtain and compare current icing PIREPS and AIRMET ZULU for areas of the U.S. where CIP/FIP shows a high likelihood of significant icing.

EXERCISE 16:

AVIATION WEATHER FORECASTS

OBJECTIVES:
- To familiarize you with common alphanumeric aviation weather forecast information
- To familiarize you with common graphical aviation weather forecast information

References: *Aviation Weather*, Chapter 16, "Aviation Weather Resources"; Chapter 17, "Weather Evaluation for Flight"; and Appendix D, "Standard Meteorological Codes and Graphics for Aviation." Supplemental reading: *AC 00-45F, Aviation Weather Services*, Sections 4 and 7.

BACKGROUND DISCUSSION

The current weather conditions are provided by the latest METARs, surface and constant pressure analyses charts, radar reports and summaries, and weather depiction charts. This information is extremely important for safe flight **now**. On the other hand, good flight **planning** requires an understanding of weather conditions in the future; that is, **forecast** information.

Weather forecasting is inexact for a number of reasons, including inadequate observations of current conditions and the inability to resolve small-scale phenomena, such as a single turbulent eddy. In order to handle these imperfections, the smart user will proactively work to maximize the forecast accuracy. You can do this by knowing the forecast products: What is predicted? When is it predicted to occur? Where is it predicted — location, area, and/or altitude? How long can the prediction be used? As you answer these questions, keep some critical rules of thumb in mind.

- The accuracy of every forecast deteriorates as more time passes since the forecast was made. **(Be sure you have the most recent forecast.)**
- When the weather is bad, forecast accuracy deteriorates even more rapidly as a forecast "ages." **(Be sure you have the most recent forecast.)**

In this exercise, you will practice interpreting a variety of forecast information, including terminal aerodrome forecasts (TAFs), area forecasts (FAs), and significant weather prognostic charts. Before you begin, you should have thoroughly read the related chapters and reviewed Appendix D in *Aviation Weather*.

TASK 16-1: TERMINAL AERODROME FORECAST (TAF).

A terminal aerodrome forecast (TAF) is a statement of predicted weather conditions for a specific airport over a specific period of time (usually 24 hours). Although the TAF code is adopted internationally, each country is allowed certain variations. The code presented here is the version used in the United States. By design, the meteorological elements of the TAF code and METAR code are the same. Additionally, TAF has information about the beginning and ending of the forecast period, non-convective wind shear (WS), probability (PROB) of certain events, and forecast descriptors such as "from" (FM) and "temporarily" (TEMPO). A TAF code breakdown is given in Appendix D in *Aviation Weather*.

In this task, you are given two TAFs for interpretation. Review the coding and answer the questions that follow each forecast.

```
TAF
KSYR 241735Z 241818 08008KT P6SM BKN250
     FM2200 12012KT P6SM BKN120 OVC250
     FM0200 14014KT P6SM BKN040 OVC120
      TEMPO 0305 3SM -FZRA OVC025
     FM0500 14014KT 3SM -FZRA OVC015
      TEMPO 0509 1SM FZRA BR OVC008
     FM0900 14014KT 3SM -RA BR OVC009
      TEMPO 0911 1SM -FZRA BR OVC005
     FM1100 17012KT 3SM -RA BR OVC009
      TEMPO 1116 1SM -RA BR OVC005
     FM1600 25012KT 3SM BR OVC025
      TEMPO 1618 1SM -RA BR OVC008=
```

1. Message type _____, ICAO station location _____.

2. Issue date ___, time _____ Z, local standard time _____.

3. Valid Period: Beginning date ____, time _____Z.

    Ending date ____,   time _____Z.

4. Initial conditions (in plain language):

5. What will the meteorological conditions be at the **end** of the forecast period (in plain language)?

6. This TAF reflects conditions during an approaching warm front at Syracuse, NY. Evidence of the frontal type is found in the wind, sky, and weather conditions, as well as their changes over the forecast period. Explain the evidence in the following space. A sketch may help.

7. When will the conditions first become MVFR?

8. When will the conditions first become IFR?

9. When will the conditions improve from IFR to MVFR?

10. In addition to IMC, what other aviation weather hazard(s) are forecast to occur during the TAF period?

Use the following TAF to answer questions 11 through 15.

```
            ZCZC LAXTAFBUR
            TTAA00 KLAX 241700
            TAF
            KBUR 241725Z 241818 33010KT P6SM SKC
                    TEMPO 2004 35014G20KT
                    FM0400 35010KT P6SM SKC WS015/03035KT
                    TEMPO 1018 35015G25KT=

            NNNN
```

11. Message type _____, ICAO station location _____.

12. Issue date ___, time _____ Z, local standard time _____.

13. Valid Period: Beginning date ____, time _____Z.

             Ending date ____,   time _____Z.

NAME: _____

DATE: _____ CLASS: _____

14. What will the meteorological conditions be at the **end** of the forecast period?

15. This TAF is characteristic of a "Santa Ana" condition over Southern California. A strong high-pressure area over the interior deserts, coupled with a northerly flow aloft, causes the winds to blow toward the coast. A mountain wave develops with clear skies over the mountains north and east of Los Angeles. At the surface, dry, gusty, northerly or northeasterly winds prevail, especially along the south- and southwest-facing mountain slopes. This particular case is a winter Santa Ana; strong radiational cooling of the ground at night causes the layer of air near the surface to stabilize. The result is that the surface winds weaken, but gusty mountain winds continue aloft. This scenario demonstrates an important aviation weather hazard that is illustrated on one line of the KBUR terminal forecast. Give a plain language description of the hazardous condition mentioned in this TAF. Refer to all relevant time periods in terms of **local standard time**.

TASK 16-2: AREA FORECAST (FA), AIRMET (WA).

An area forecast (FA) is a forecast of general weather conditions over an area the size of several states. It is used to determine forecasts of weather enroute and forecasts for airports where TAFs are not issued. Figure 16-1 shows the six FA forecast areas in the contiguous United States. More details about FAs are given in the references for this exercise.

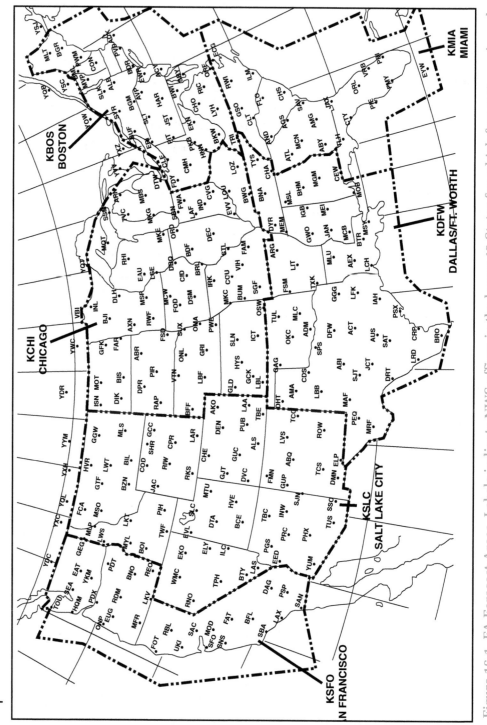

Figure 16-1. FA Forecast Areas. Labels indicate NWS offices in the lower 48 States for which forecasts are issued by the Aviation Weather Center (AWC).

In this task, you will review the general properties of an FA, and then apply that knowledge to interpret an actual area forecast. An FA contains a **Communication and Products Header** section, a **Precautionary Statement** section, a **Synopsis** section, and a **VFR Clouds and Weather** section.

1. Give a general description of the information you would find in the synopsis section.

2. Give a general description of the information you would find in the VFR clouds and Weather section.

3. What important aviation weather information is **not** found in area forecasts? Where do you find it?

4. Define an AIRMET.

5. An FA is **always** used in conjunction with an AIRMET SIERRA. Define AIRMET SIERRA.

6. Define AIRMET TANGO.

7. Define AIRMET ZULU.

8. In an FA, heights may be given as above sea level or above ground level. How can you tell if a height is AGL or MSL? When a height is given, what must be done to decode the height to plain language?

9. How long is the forecast period for an area forecast?

10. How often are FAs issued?

The following is an actual FA for the West Coast of the U.S. Use it to answer questions 11 through 16. You also may want to refer to figure 8-4 in this manual to help you identify specific geographical areas. Note common abbreviations in the FA, such as "TROF" for trough, "CDFNT" for cold front, "CSTL" for coastal, "MOD" for moderate, "STG" for strong. Common METAR/TAF abbreviations and postal codes for various states are used throughout the FA. The three letter identifiers mentioned in the FA denote locations given on figure 16-2.

```
ZCZC MKCFA6W
FAUS6 KSFO 261045
SFOC FA 261045
SYNOPSIS AND VFR CLDS/WX
SYNOPSIS VALID UNTIL 270500
CLDS/WX VALID UNTIL 262300...OTLK VALID 262300-270500
WA OR CA AND CSTL WTRS
.
SEE AIRMET SIERRA FOR IFR CONDS AND MTN OBSCN.
TS IMPLY SEV OR GTR TURB SEV ICE LLWS AND IFR CONDS.
NON MSL HGTS DENOTED BY AGL OR CIG.
.
SYNOPSIS
ALF...11Z STG LOW W OF VANCOUVER ISLAND..WITH TROF TO W OF WA/OR
   CSTL WTRS. MOD-STG SWLY FLOW WA/OR..BECMG MOD WSWLY OVR NRN CA.
   05Z TROF AXIS NR FCA-PIH LN. MOD-STG W/WNWLY FLOW WA/OR..LGT-
   MOD NRN CA.
SFC..11Z CDFNT OVR ERN WA TO PDT-LKV-NRN CA CST BTN FOT/UKI. LOW
   PRES /RMNS OF NORA/ CNTRD IN SWRN UT. 05Z CDFNT THRU NERN TIP
   MT-COD-EKO-RNO-SAC TO CA CST JUST N SFO.
.
WA CASCDS WWD
CSTLN..BKN025 OVC035 TOP FL200. VIS 3-5SM -RA. ISOL TSRA. TS TOPS
   FL320. 14Z SCT025 BKN040 BKN060..WITH -SHRA. ISOL TSRA. OTLK...
   MVFR CIG SHRA.
ELSW..SCT-BKN020-030 BKN060 TOP FL200. SCT -SHRA/SHRA. ISOL TSRA.
   TS TOPS FL320. 18Z BKN030. SCT VIS 3-5SM -SHRA/SHRA. OTLK...
   MVFR CIG SHRA.
.
WA E OF CASCDS
WRN HLF..BKN-OVC100-120 TOP FL200. ISOL TSRA. TS TOPS FL320. 16Z
   SCT100-120 BKN200. ISOL TSRA. OTLK...VFR.
ERN HLF..BKN-SCT080 BKN-OVC140 TOP FL200. WDLY SCT -SHRA. ISOL-
   WDLY SCT TSRA. TS TOPS FL350. 16Z SCT080 BKN110. WDLY SCT
   -SHRA. ISOL TSRA. OTLK...VFR.
.
```

NAME: _____

DATE: _____ CLASS: _____

```
OR CASCDS WWD
CSTLN..SCT-BKN015 BKN-OVC040 TOP FL180. VIS 3-5SM -RA BR. OCNL
   RA. SRN PTN WDLY SCT -SHRA. 14Z SCT-BKN025 BKN-SCT040. WDLY SCT
   -SHRA/SHRA. 20Z SCT-BKN025 BKN-SCT040. WDLY SCT -SHRA. OTLK...
   VFR.
SWRN INTR..SCT-BKN070 BKN110 TOP FL180. ISOL-WDLY SCT -SHRA. 18Z
   SCT070. OTLK...VFR.
ELSW..SCT-BKN020-025 OVC035-055 TOP FL200. WDLY SCT -SHRA. 18Z
   SCT-BKN025-035 BKN060. WDLY SCT -SHRA. OTLK...VFR SHRA.
   .
OR E OF CASCDS
WRN HLF..SCT120 BKN150-180 TOP FL200. 20Z SCT-BKN100. OTLK...VFR.
ERN HLF..SCT110-130 SCT-BKN150 BKN200. 15Z SCT140-160. 18Z SCT-
   BKN130-160 TOP FL200. OTLK...VFR.
   .
NRN CA...SFO-SAC-RNO LN NWD
CSTL SXN
   NRN CSTLN..BKN-SCT010 TOP 120. VIS 3-5SM BR. ISOL-WDLY SCT
      -SHRA. 16Z SCT015 BKN025. OTLK...VFR.
   ELSW..SCT-BKN015 BKN035 TOP 120. 16Z SCT015. OTLK...VFR.
SAC VLY..SKC. NRN PTN SCT100 TIL 13Z. OTLK...VFR.
MTNS..SCT-BKN100 TOP 160. 18Z SCT090-100. OTLK...VFR.
   .

CNTRL CA
CSTL SXN
   SFO BAY AREA..SCT-BKN010-015 TOP 030. 18Z SCT015-020. 20Z SKC.
      OTLK...VFR.
ELSW..BKN-SCT010-020 TOP 030. 18Z SKC. OTLK...VFR.
SAN JOAQUIN VLY..SKC. OCNL SCT100 TIL 20Z. OTLK...VFR.
MTNS..SCT-BKN100 TOP 150. 15Z SCT100 SCT200. 20Z SKC. OTLK...VFR.
   .

SRN CA..SBA-BFL-60NNW TPH LN SWD
CSTL SXN..SCT-BKN010-015 BKN-SCT025 BKN060-080 TOP 150. OCNL VIS
   3-5SM BR. 16Z SCT020 SCT080. 21Z SKC OR SCT CI. OTLK...VFR.
INTR MTNS/DESERTS..SCT-BKN040 BKN070-080 TOP 160. 17Z SCT070
   SCT200. OTLK...VFR.
   .
CSTL WTRS
WA/OR WTRS...SCT-BKN015-025 BKN040-060 TOP120. ISOL-WDLY SCT
   -SHRA. ISOL TSRA. TS TOPS FL300. OTLK...VFR.
NRN CA..SCT-BKN015-025 BKN-OVC040-060 TOP 150. ISOL -SHRA.
   OTLK...VFR.
CNTRL CA WTRS..SCT-BKN015-025 TOP 050. OTLK...VFR.
SRN CA WTRS..SCT-BKN015-025 BKN050-070 TOP 120. OTLK...VFR.
....
```

11. Use the information in the **synopsis section** of the SFOC FA to locate and draw the major surface and upper air features on figure 16-2 at 11Z (left) and 18 hours later at 05Z (right). Neatness will clarify results. Use contrasting colors to differentiate between levels (red: surface, blue: aloft). For conditions aloft (ALF), indicate the location of each trough line (or axis) with heavy dashed lines. Again, place 11Z conditions on the left-hand diagram and 05Z conditions on the right. Show the direction of flow with thick

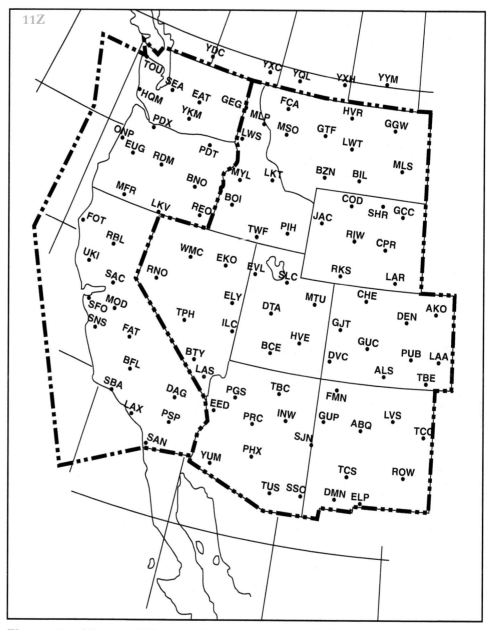

Figure 16-2. Western U.S. Area Forecast Map. (11Z left); 05Z (right)

NAME: _____

DATE: _____ CLASS: _____

arrows for strong flow and thin arrows for weak flow. For surface (SFC) conditions, indicate fronts with color coded lines and circulation centers as a block "L" or "H," whichever is appropriate.

12. The subsections in the **VFR clouds and weather section** of the FA correspond to the geographical areas of the particular office responsible for issuing that section of the FA. Use figure 16-2 (left) to locate and (optional) neatly draw the boundaries of each of the geographical areas.

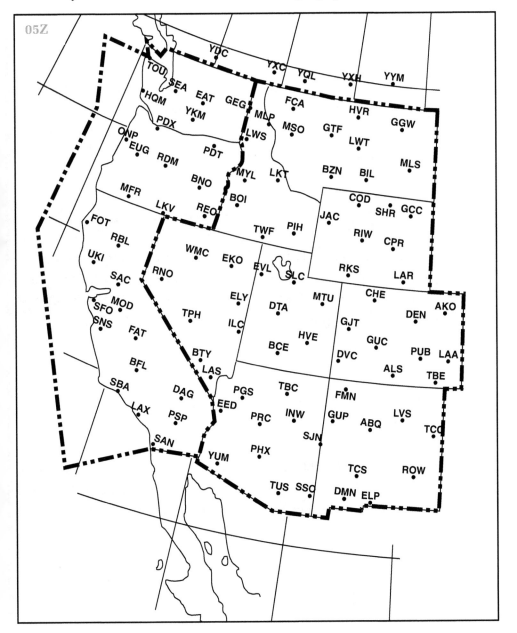

13. Read all of the sections on VFR clouds and weather. Do you see any relation between the winds, clouds, and precipitation described in this section and the location of surface and upper air features (lows, highs, fronts, troughs, etc.) described in the synopsis section? Briefly describe the relationship below.

14. Give a plain language description of conditions in the area along the coastline of Washington, west of the Cascades after 0600 PST.

15. AIRMET SIERRA, referred to in the KSFO FA, is given on the next page. In the space provided, describe in plain language the **specific** added information that is included in the AIRMET. (Optional) Locate and label the affected area(s) on Figure 16-2 (previous page).

16. AIRMETs TANGO and ZULU are given on the next page for the forecast area. In the space provided, write brief, plain language interpretations. (Optional) Locate and label the referenced areas on figure 16-2 (previous two pages).

NAME: _____

DATE: _____ CLASS: _____

```
WAUS1 KSFO 261345
SFOS WA 261345
AIRMET SIERRA UPDT 2 FOR IFR AND MTN OBSCN VALID UNTIL 262000
.
NO SGFNT IFR EXP.
.
AIRMET MTN OBSCN...WA OR CA
FROM YDC TO RDM TO FOT TO ONP TO HQM TO TOU TO YDC
MTNS OBSCD BY CLDS/PCPN. CONDS CONTG BYD 20Z THRU 02Z.
.
AIRMET MTN OBSCN...CA
FROM RBL TO 30E RBL TO EED TO YUM TO SAN TO LAX TO 25E BFL TO RBL
MTNS OBSCD BY CLDS. CONDS ENDG 16-18Z.
....=
```

```
WAUS1 KSFO 261345
SFOT WA 261345
AIRMET TANGO UPDT 2 FOR TURB VALID UNTIL 262000
.
AIRMET TURB...WA OR AND CSTL WTRS ID MT WY NV UT
FROM YQL TO SHR TO RIW TO UKI TO 120W FOT TO 120W TOU TO YQL
MOD TURB BLW 160.  CONDS CONT BYD 20Z THRU 02Z.
....=




WAUS1 KSFO 261345
SFOZ WA 261345
AIRMET ZULU UPDT 2 FOR ICE AND FRZLVL VALID UNTIL 262000
.
AIRMET ICE...WA
FROM YXC TO HQM TO TOU TO YXC
MOD ICE BTN 070 AND 170. CONDS ENDG 20Z.
.
FRZLVL..WA...WRN...060-070.  ERN...070-110 BECMG 065-090 BY 21Z.
        OR...NWRN..065-090.  NERN...110-125 BECMG 080-110 BY 21Z.
            SWRN...090-130.  SERN...110-135.
        CA...NRN 130-160.  CNTRL..160-175.  SRN...150-170.
....=
```

TASK 16-3: LOW-LEVEL SIGNIFICANT WEATHER PROGNOSTIC CHARTS.

Graphical presentations of aviation weather forecasts give you a "snapshot" of expected conditions over the area of interest. One of the most common presentations of this type is the significant weather prognostic chart, shown in figure 16-3. This task gives you practice in interpreting the low-level version of this chart for the U.S. Review the section on this topic on pages 16-19 and 16-20 as well as Appendix D, page D-23 in *Aviation Weather* **before** proceeding.

1. Examine the four-panel chart presented in figure 16-3. In the space below, describe what the **upper right-hand panel** represents and give the valid date and time in UTC.

2. In the space below, describe what the **lower left-hand panel** represents and give the valid date and time in UTC.

3. The upper panels cover what altitude range? (Express in feet, MSL)

4. Define "valid time (VT)"

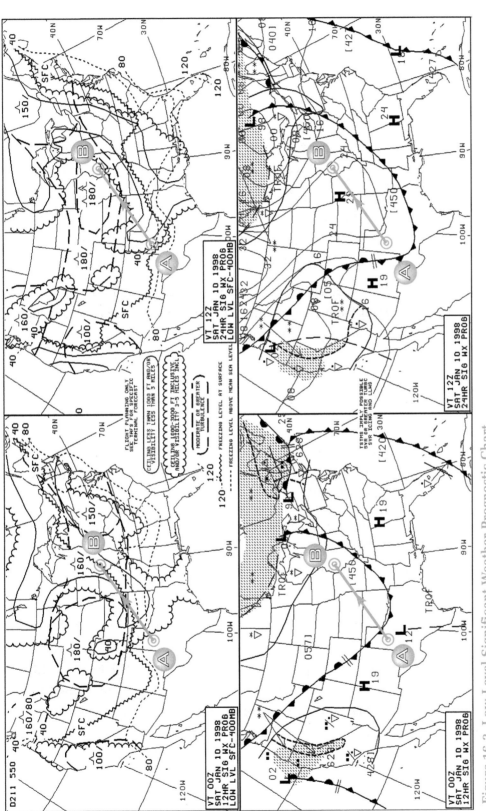

Figure 16-3. Low-Level Significant Weather Prognostic Chart.

CAUTION: The Significant Weather Prognostic Chart is for flight planning only.

5. Over what time period can the upper right-hand panel be used for flight planning purposes?

6. The significant weather prognostic chart is a forecast map, as opposed to an "analysis chart." When were the forecasts made for the charts in figure 16-3? (date/time) _____/_____Z

7. In the upper **left-hand** panel, without obliterating any data, **highlight** the 8,000-foot and surface freezing level lines. Trace the **outline** of the MVFR areas in red pencil. Then, **shade** the IFR areas with the red pencil.

8. Provide a plain language explanation of the numbers and symbols over IA in the upper **right-hand** panel. With an ordinary pencil, lightly shade the area where those numbers and symbols apply.

9. In both of the lower panels, without obliterating any data, color code the fronts according to their types. Also highlight low-pressure centers (RED L) and high centers (BLUE H).

10. The isobars in the lower panels in figure 16-3 are drawn at _____ mb intervals. The isobars on a typical surface analysis chart (not shown) are drawn at _____mb intervals.

Use the following scenario and figure 16-3 to answer questions 11 through 15. You are planning a flight from Lubbock, TX to Peoria, IL. The estimated flight time is 3.5 hours. Your departure is tentatively scheduled for 1600 CST on January 9, 1998. You would like to fly at 8,000 feet MSL. Your flight track is shown as a thick, black line (A-B) on each of the panels in figure 16-3. You are instrument-rated and current.

NAME: _____

DATE: _____ CLASS: _____

11. Circle the date/time labels of the panels that are closest to the time of your flight.

12. List the predicted weather hazards along your flight track.

13. Is icing possible? Why? If so, where would you expect to find it along your track?

14. Will conditions anywhere along your planned flight track be improving or worsening during the flight? If so, what conditions? Where? Why?

15. How can you modify your flight plan to minimize the hazards you have listed in question **12** and **13**?

QUESTIONS

1. Give plain language interpretations of the following TAFs.

```
    TTAA00 KATL 242057 AAB
    TAF AMD
    KATL 242057Z 242118 09012KT 1/2SM FG OVC001
          TEMPO 2124 1SM BR OVC006
          FM0000 14012KT 5SM BR SCT006 OVC105
          TEMPO 0004 2SM BR OVC005
          FM0400 19010KT 5SM BKN025
          FM0600 24008KT P6SM SCT035
          FM1400 29008KT P6SM SCT035 BKN250=


    TTAA00 KTUS 241741
    TAF
    KTUS 241730Z 241818 15008KT P6SM SCT060 BKN100
          FM2000 20012KT P6SM SCT060 BKN100
          TEMPO 2002 -SHRA BKN060
          FM0200 25010KT P6SM -RA SCT030 BKN050
          TEMPO 0207 5SM RA BKN030
          FM0700 25006KT P6SM -SHRA SCT030 BKN050
          TEMPO 0712 5SM -RASN BKN030
          FM1200 VRB05KT 5SM -RASN FEW010 SCT030 BKN050
          FM1400 VRB05KT P6SM FEW010 SCT030 BKN050=


    TTAA00 KMSP 241731
    TAF
    KMSP 241725Z 241818 15006KT 5SM BR OVC006
          FM2000 VRB05KT P6SM OVC012
          TEMPO 2001 OVC008
          FM0100 33007KT P6SM OVC008
          TEMPO 0104 OVC012=
```

KATL:

KTUS:

KMSP:

2. What is a TWEB route forecast? Describe its format.

3. How many times per day are TAFs issued. What are those times (Z)?

4. Carefully define and describe the following weather products.

FB:

CWA:

MIS:

5. What are **high level significant weather prognostic charts**? In your definition, include the area covered, altitude range, specific weather information provided, and the times of issuance.

6. What are SIGMETs and CONVECTIVE SIGMETs? Describe their formats and what types of weather phenomena they cover. (Optional) What are the criteria for the issuance of <u>International</u> SIGMETs?

EXERCISE 17:

WEATHER EVALUATION FOR FLIGHT

OBJECTIVES:

- To apply the information learned in this Laboratory Manual
- To use a combination of products to evaluate the weather
- To practice the weather-related decision making process

References: *Aviation Weather*, Chapter 16, "Aviation Weather Resources"; Chapter 17, "Weather Evaluation for Flight"; and Appendix D, "Standard Meteorological Codes and Graphics for Aviation." Supplemental reading: *AC 00-45E, Aviation Weather Services*, most sections.

BACKGROUND DISCUSSION

The "self-briefing procedure" described in Chapter 17 of *Aviation Weather* is the basis of this exercise. Figure 17-1 summarizes the procedure in the form of a flow diagram. This exercise uses a scenario-based flight to help you practice the evaluation of weather in a realistic setting. You will enter the briefing process at the "preflight evaluation" stage. (See figure 17-1.) It is assumed that you have completed the overview and general assessment of the weather situation 24 hours prior to the flight. You will now make a detailed evaluation within a few hours of the proposed departure time (the "preflight evaluation"). Your objective is to evaluate that information to reach a "go," "no-go," or "modified flight plan" decision for the proposed flight. You are given the flight description and a collection of graphical and alphanumeric weather information.

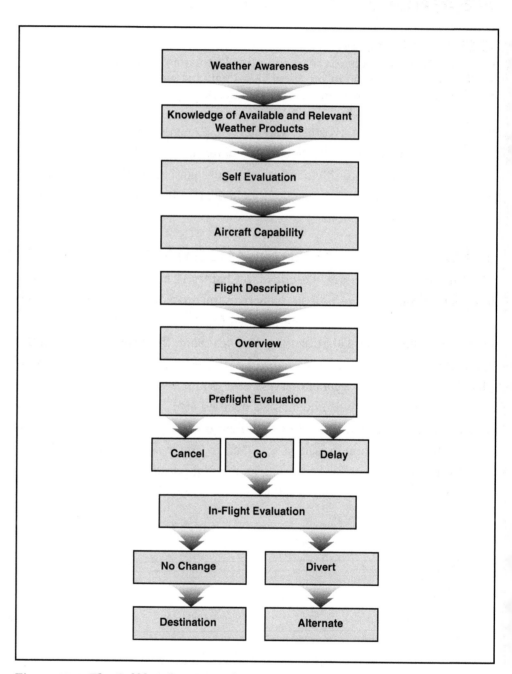

Figure 17-1. The Self-briefing Procedure.

NAME: _____

DATE: _____ CLASS: _____

TASKS 17-1: THE SCENARIO.

In order to get the most out of this exercise, evaluate the information as it becomes available; that is, in the order it is presented in this exercise. Each task is identified with a local time that indicates when the included weather information becomes available to you. This simulates, at least to some degree, your acquisition of data in real time. It also provides a more realistic sequence of questions and conclusions based on the information at hand. You will notice that the detail of information increases with the introduction of each new piece of data. You will be asked the same questions in each task. Justify your answers on the basis of each new piece of information.

You are at Birmingham, AL (BHM) planning a flight from BHM to Minneapolis, MN (MSP) via St. Louis, MO (STL). You are instrument-rated and current. Your operational ceiling is 13,500 feet and your aircraft has propeller anti-icing equipment, but no deicing boots. Your optimum flight altitude is 8,000 feet MSL and you have no oxygen equipment onboard the aircraft. Today is December 23. The tentative departure time is 1330 CST. Taking winds aloft into consideration (GS 160 knots), the estimated time enroute is 2:15 to STL and another 2:30 to MSP. You will spend one hour on the ground at STL.

Place your flight track on the plotting chart in figure 17-2. You will refer to this chart in other tasks in this exercise.

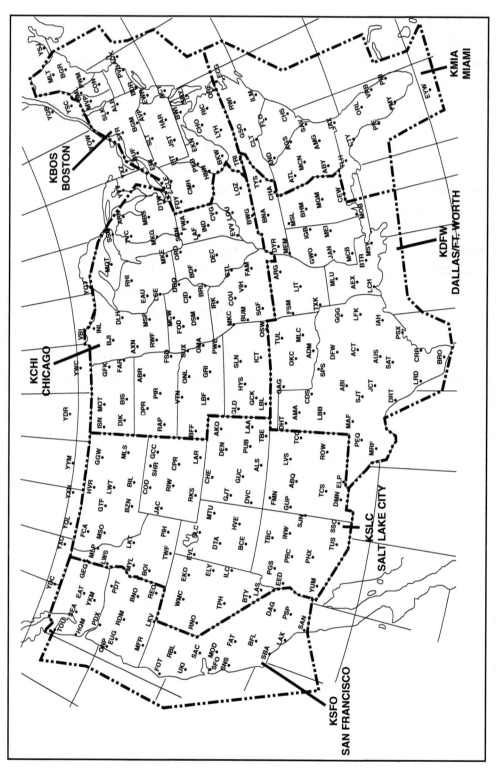

Figure 17-2. Plotting Chart.

TASK 17-2: 0630 CST, DECEMBER 23.

It is now 0630 CST. Over the last 24 hours, you have followed the general weather conditions over the route. The development of these conditions is shown in the 12- and 24-hour significant weather prognostic charts (SIG WX PROG) in figure 17-3. For convenience, the location of your proposed flight is shown on each map.

1. What and where are the potentially hazardous weather conditions at the time of your proposed departure and along the track of your flight?

2. Would you modify your flight plan at this point? How?

3. If you elect a "no-go" at this point, explain why and continue with the exercise to confirm your decision.

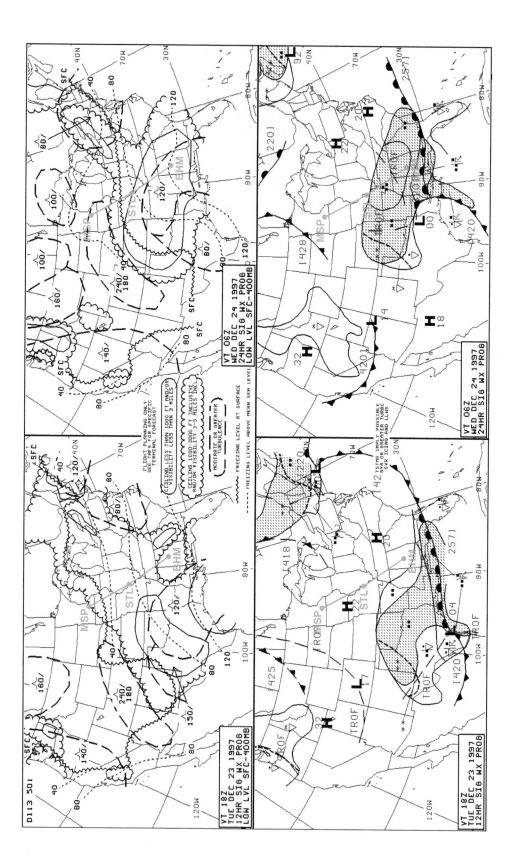

Figure 17-3. Weather available to you at 0630 CST.

TASK 17-3: 0800 CST, DECEMBER 23.

The most recent FAs for KCHI and KDFW are now available with AIRMETS SIERRA, TANGO, and ZULU. For your information, the areas of forecast responsibility for KCHI and KDFW are shown in figure 17-2. Also available are the latest surface, 300 mb, and weather depiction charts, as well as the latest IR satellite image. These are shown in figure 17-4.

1. What and where are the potentially hazardous weather conditions at the time of your proposed departure and along the track of your flight?

2. Would you modify your flight plan at this point? How?

3. If you elect a "no-go" at this point, explain why and continue with the exercise to confirm your decision.

```
DFWC FA 231300 AMD
SYNOPSIS AND VFR CLDS/WX
SYNOPSIS VALID UNTIL 240500
CLDS/WX VALID UNTIL 232300...OTLK VALID 232300-240500
OK TX AR TN LA MS AL AND CSTL WTRS
.
SEE AIRMET SIERRA FOR IFR CONDS AND MTN OBSCN.
TS IMPLY SEV OR GTR TURB SEV ICE LLWS AND IFR CONDS.
NON MSL HGTS DENOTED BY AGL OR CIG.
.
SYNOPSIS...SFC LOW DVLPG OVER FAR W TX. AFT 15Z IT WILL BGM MOVG
EWD 15KT TO OVER E CNTRL TX BY 05Z. WMFNT AND CDFNT DVLPG AS LOW
INTSFYS AND AT 05Z WMFNT LCTD FROM LOW TO SERN LA AND CDFNT TO
OFFSHR SERN TX.
.
OK ...UPDT...
CIG OVC030. SCT -SHRA. TOPS FL200. 13Z CIG OVC010 VIS 3-5SM  -RA
BR. TOPS LYRD TO FL250. WDLY SCT -TSRA SRN OK TOPS FL350 TIL 21Z.
TS OCNL IN LNS/CLUSTERS. OTLK...IFR CIG SN BR FG.
.
NWRN TX ...UPDT...
CIG OVC010 VIS 3-5SM -RA -FZRA -SN BR. TOPS LYRD TO FL250. SCT
TSRA TOPS FL350 TIL 18Z. TS OCNL IN LNS/CLUSTERS. OTLK...IFR CIG
SN BR FG.
.
SWRN TX ...UPDT...
CIG BKN010 VIS 3-5SM -RA BR. TOPS LYRD TO FL250. SCT TSRA TOPS
FL350 TIL 18Z. TS OCNL IN LNS/CLUSTERS. OTLK...IFR CIG RA SN BR
FG.
.
N CNTRL TX ...UPDT...
CIG OVC030. SCT -SHRA. TOPS FL200. 13Z CIG OVC010 VIS 3-5SM -RA
BR. TOPS LYRD TO FL250. SCT TSRA TOPS FL350 TIL 21Z. TS IN
LNS/CLUSTERS. OTLK...IFR CIG RA BR FG.
.
NERN TX ...UPDT...
CIG BKN050 OVC090. TOPS LYRD TO FL250. 18Z CIG OVC 010 VIS 3-5SM
-RA BR. TOPS LYRD TO FL250. WDLY SCT TSRA TOPS FL350. TS IN
LNS/CLUSTERS. OTLK... IFR CIG RA BR FG.
.
SERN TX ...UPDT...
CIG OVC020 LYR TOP FL250. SCT TSRA...POSS SEV. CB TOP FL450.
OTLK...MVFR CIG.
.
S CNTRL TX ...UPDT...
CIG OVC015 LYR TOP FL250. WDLY SCT TSRA...POSS SEV N HLF. CB TOP
FL450. 23Z SKC. OTLK... VFR.
.
AR
```

Figure 17-4. Weather available to you at 0800 CST.

NAME: _____

DATE: _____ CLASS: _____

```
NRN HLF...CIG OVC015 VIS 3-5SM BR. TOP 060. 20Z CIG OVC010 VIS 3-
5SM -RA BR FG. TOPS LYRD TO FL250. OTLK... IFR CIG RA BR FG.
SRN HLF...CIG BKN050 OVC090. TOPS LYRD TO FL250. 20Z CIG OVC 010
VIS 3-5SM -RA BR. TOPS LYRD TO FL250. WDLY SCT -TSRA TOPS FL350.
OTLK... IFR CIG RA BR FG.
.
LA ...UPDT...
NRN HLF...CIG BKN050 OVC090 TOP LYRD TO FL250 BECMG 20Z CIG
OVC010 VIS 3-5SM -RA BR. WDLY SCT TSRA..POSS SEV. CB TOP FL450.
OTLK... IFR CIG RA BR FG.
SRN HLF...CIG OVC030 LYR TOP FL250. SCT TSRA..POSS SEV. CB TOP
FL450. OTLK...IFR CIG RA BR FG.
.
TN
CIG OVC015 OCNL VIS 3-5SM BR. TOP 050. OTLK...MVFR CIG.
.
MS ...UPDT...
EXTRM N...CIG OVC015 OCNL VIS 3-5SM BR. TOP 050. OTLK...MVFR CIG.
RMNDR...CIG OVC090 LYR TOP FL250. SCT TSRA...POSS SEV. CB TOP
FL450. OTLK...IFR CIG RA BR FG.
.
AL ...UPDT...
N QTR...CIG BKN-SCT015 LYR TOP FL250. VIS 3-5SM BR. 16-18Z AGL
SCT025 BKN120. OTLK...VFR RA.
S QTR...CIG OVC050 LYR TOP FL250 LWRG 17Z CIG BKN020-030. WDLY
SCT -SHRA/TSRA W PTNS SPRDG THRUT BY 16-18Z. TS POSS SEV. CB TOP
FL450. OTLK...MVFR CIG.
RMNDR...CIG OVC080 LYR TOP FL250. TIL 16Z VIS 3-5SM BR AND OCNL
CIG BKN010 E HLF.
.
CSTL WTRS
OVC020. WDLY SCT -TSRA TOPS FL400. OTLK...VFR S TX CSTL WTRS.
MVFR CIG ELSW.
....

NNNN
```

```
WAUS1 KDFW
AIRMET SIERRA FOR IFR AND MTN OBSCN VALID UNTIL 232100
.
AIRMET IFR...OK TX AR LA MS AL CSTL WTRS ...UPDT...
FROM OSW TO ARG TO TXK TO MEI TO CHA TO 50SW ABY TO 40W CEW TO
180SSW CEW TO 130SSW LCH TO 70E BRO TO 50W BRO TO DRT TO ELP TO
40W MAF TO DHT TO 50W LBL TO OSW
CIG BLW 010/VIS BLW 3SM PCPN/BR/FG. CONDS WDSPRD NW TX AND
WRN HLF OK. CONDS ENDG S HLF S CNTRL TX AND NRN AL 17-19Z. CONDS
CONTG BYD 21Z THRU 03Z ELSW.
...UPDT TO COMBINE AREAS/ADD PTNS OF MS/CONT CONDS NRN AL TIL 19Z
.
AIRMETS MTN OBSCN...TN KY
FROM HNN TO TRI TO CHA TO LOZ TO HNN
MTNS OBSC CLDS/PCPN/BR. CONDS CONTG BYD 21Z THRU 03Z.
.
AIRMETS MTN OBSCN...TX
FROM 40NW PEQ TO 80S MRF TO ELP TO 40NW PEQ
MTNS OBSC CLDS/PCPN/BR. CONDS CONTG BYD 21Z THRU 03Z.
....=

NNNN
```

```
WAUS1 KDFW
AIRMET TANGO FOR TURB VALID UNTIS 232100
.
AIRMET TURB...OK TX AR LA TN MS AL
FROM OSW TO ARG TO TRI TO CHA TO 5ONW ABY TO GGG TO SAT TO 80S
MRF TO ELP TO 40W MAF TO DHT TO 50W LBL TO OSW
MOD TURB BTN FL240 AND FL380. CONDS CONTG BYD 21Z THRU 03Z.
.
ELSW NO SGFNT TURB EXP EXC VCY CNVTV ACT.
....=
```

```
WAUS1 KDFW
AIRMET ZULU FOR ICE AND FRZLVL VALID UNTIL 232100
.
AIRMET ICE...OK TX AK LA MS AL TN
FROM OSW TO ARG TO 20N BNA TO MGM TO DFW TO DRT TO 80S MRF TO ELP
TO 40W MAF TO DHT TO 50W LBL TO OSW
MOD ICE BTN FRZLVL AND FL220. FRZLVL SFC-040 OK/TX PNHDLS AND
N 2/3S TX S PLAINS SLPG 080-120 SE OF A 40W MAF-SPS-GAG LN.
MULT FRZLVLS 020-095 OVR OK. CONDS CONTG BYD 21Z THRU 03Z.
ELSW NO SGFNT ICE EXP OUTSIDE CNVTV ACT.
.
FRZLVL...SFC-040 OK/TX PNHDLS AND N 2/3S TX S PLAINS SLPG 080 ALG
A 40W MAF-SPS-GAG LN SLPG 120-140 SE LRD-AUS-AEX-GWO-ABY LN. MULT
FRZLVLS 020-095 OVR OK EXC PNHDLS.
....=
```

NAME: _____

DATE: _____ CLASS: _____

```
CHIC FA 231355 AMD
SYNOPSIS AND VFR CLDS/WX
SYNOPSIS VALID UNTIL 240500
CLDS/WX VALID UNTIL 232300...OTLK VALID 232300-240500
ND SD NE KS MN IA MO WI LM LS MI LH IL IN KY

.
SEE AIRMET SIERRA FOR IFR CONDS AND MTN OBSCN.
TS IMPLY SEV OR GTR TURB SEV ICE LLWS AND IFR CONDS.
NON MSL HGTS DENOTED BY AGL OR CIG.

.
SYNOPSIS...HIGH PRES RDG ACRS CNTRL NE TO NERN AR. RDG WILL MOV
EWD TO ACRS MI/ERN KY BY 05Z. CDFNT FCST TO MOV INTO WRN ND ABT
21Z AND MOV TO A NWRN MN-NERN CO LN BY 05Z

.
ND SD
SKC. OTLK... MVFR CIG ERN QTR. VFR ELSW.

.
NE
ERN THIRD...CIG OVC020 TOP 040. OTLK... IFR CIG BR FG.
RMNDR...SKC. OTLK... VFR.

.
KS ...UPDT...
ERN THIRD...CIG OVC020. TOP 040. 17-19Z CIG OVC010 VIS 3-5SM -RA
BR FG. TOPS LYRD TO FL250. OTLK... IFR CIG RA BR FG.
SWRN AND S CNTRL...CIG OVC030. SCT -SHRA. TOPS FL200. 18Z CIG
OVC010 VIS 3-5SM -RA -SN BR. TOPS LYRD TO FL250. OTLK... IFR CIG
SN BR FG.
N CNTRL...SKC. 18Z CIG OVC030. SCT -SHRA. TOPS FL200. 21Z CIG
OVC015 VIS 3-5SM -RA -SN BR. TOPS LYRD TO FL250. OTLK... IFR CIG
SN BR FG.
NWRN...BKN150 TOP FL250. OCNL BKN100. OTLK...VFR.

.
MN
NERN QTR...CIG OVC015 VIS 3-5SM BR. TOP 040. 15Z SKC. OTLK...
MVFR CIG.
SERN QTR...CIG OVC015 VIS 3-5SM BR. TOP 040. OTLK... MVFR CIG.
WRN HLF...SKC. OCNL VIS 3-5SM BR TIL 15Z. OTLK... MVFR CIG.

.
IA
CIG OVC015 VIS 3-5SM BR. TOP 040. OTLK... IFR CIG BR.

.
MO ...UPDT...
SWRN QTR...CIG OVC015 VIS 3-5SM BR. TOP 060. 18-20Z CIG OVC010
VIS 3-5SM -RA BR FG. TOPS LYRD TO FL250. OTLK... IFR CIG RA BR
FG.
```

```
WAUS1 KCHI
AIRMET SIERRA FOR IFR AND MTN OBSCN VALID UNTIL 232100
.
AIRMET IFR...KS MN IA MO WI IL IN KY ...COR...
FROM DLH TO ORD TO FWA TO CVG TO HNN TO TRI TO ARG TO OSW TO 50W
LBL TO LAA TO GCK TO SLN TO PWE TO SUX TO DLH
CIG BLW 010/VIS BLW 3SM PCPN/BR/FG. CONDS CONTG BYD 21Z THRU
03Z KS/MO. CONDS ENDG 18-19Z IL/IN/WI/MN/KY AND 19-21Z IA.
     ... COR FOR ENDING TIME IN KY AND VOR POINTS...
.
AIRMET MTN OBSCN...KY TN
FROM HNN TO TRI TO CHA TO LOZ TO HNN
MTNS OCNL OBSC CLDS/PCPN/BR. CONDS CONTG BYD 21Z THRU 03Z.
....=

NNNN
```

```
WAUS1
CHIT WA
AIRMET TANGO FOR TURB VALID UNTIL 232100
.
AIRMET TURB...NE KS IA MO WI IL MI IN KY LM
FROM MKG TO FWA TO CVG TO HNN TO TRI TO ARG TO OSW TO 50W LBL TO
GLD TO BFF TO ONL TO MKG
MOD TURB BTN FL240 AND FL400.
CONDS CONTG BYD 21Z THRU 03Z.
....=

NNNN
```

```
WAUS1 KCHI
AIRMET ZULU FOR ICE AND FRZLVL VALID UNTIL 232100
.
AIRMET ICE...MI LH
FROM SSM TO YVV TO DTW TO FWA TO SSM
MOD ICE BLW 130. CONDS CONTG BYD 21Z ENDG 00Z.
.
AIRMET ICE...KS MO
FROM GLD TO STL TO 20N DYR TO ARG TO OSW TO 50W LBL TO GLD
MOD ICE BTN FRZLVL AND FL180. MULT FRZLVLS 010-085.
CONDS OVR SRN PTNS KS AT 15Z SPRDG RMNDR 18-20Z. CONDS CONTG
BYD 21Z THRU 03Z.
.
AIRMET ICE...MI WI IN LM ...UPDT...
FROM MQT TO SSM TO FWA TO CVG TO EVV TO ORD TO MSN TO MQT
MOD ICE BLW 060. CONDS ENDG 21Z.
     ...UPDT TO ADD PTNS ERN WI...
.
FRZLVL...SFC-040 NE OF A 50NW MOT-DPR-GLD-PWE-DBQ-DEC-FDY LN SLPG
080-105 SE OF A GAG-MKC-IRK-FAM-HNN LN. MULT FRZLVLS 040-080 W
HLF KS AND 010-085 E HLF AND SRN 2/3S MO.
....=

NNNN
```

NAME: _____

DATE: _____ CLASS: _____

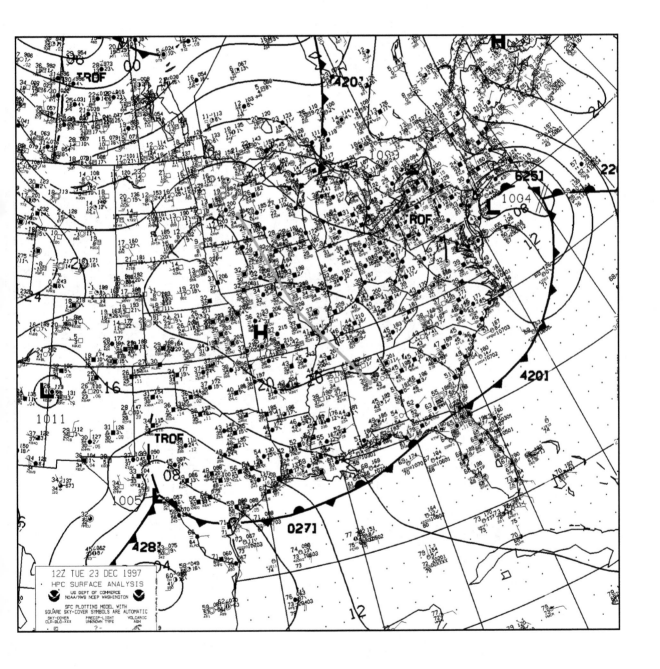

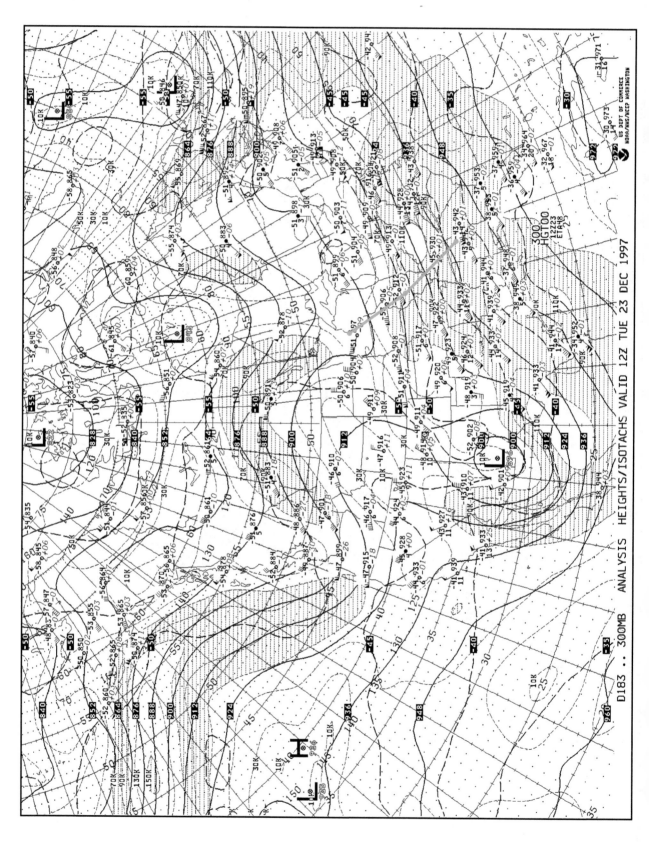

D183 •• 300MB   ANALYSIS HEIGHTS/ISOTACHS VALID 12Z TUE 23 DEC 1997

NAME: _____

DATE: _____ CLASS: _____

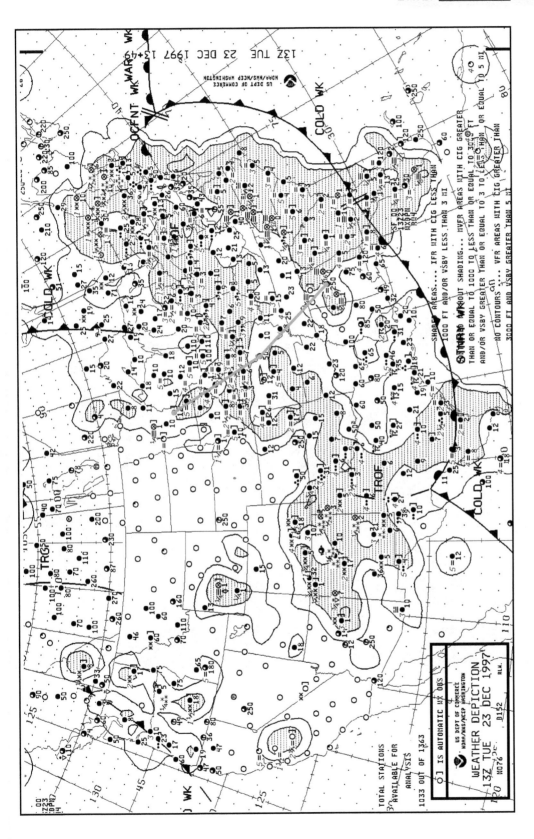

GOES 8 IR 23 DEC 97 AT 12:15 UTC

NAME: _____

DATE: _____ CLASS: _____

TASK 17-4: 0830 CST, DECEMBER 23.

You begin to focus on the actual weather conditions at several stations along your planned track. You obtain the METARs shown in figure 17-5.

1. What and where are the potentially hazardous weather conditions at the time of your proposed departure and along the track of your flight?

2. Would you modify your flight plan at this point? How?

3. If you elect a "no-go" at this point, explain why and continue with the exercise to confirm your decision.

```
KBHM 231350Z 00000KT 7SM FEW140 BKN250 04/03 A3011 RMK SLP197 T00410031=

KMEM 231352Z 36005KT 12SM OVC017 07/05 A3014 RMK SLP207 T00740051=

KSTL 231353Z 25004KT 6SM BR BKN013 OVC050 02/00 A3015 RMK AO2 SLP219 T00170000=

KMSP 231355Z 23004KT 5SM BR OVC012 M02/M04 A3007 RMK AO2 SLP194 T10221044=
```

Figure 17-5. Weather available to you at 0830 CST.

TASK 17-5: 1000 CST, DECEMBER 23.

The latest radar summary chart is available. (See Figure 17-6.)

1. What and where are the potentially hazardous weather conditions at the time of your proposed departure and along the track of your flight?

2. Would you modify your flight plan at this point? How?

3. If you elect a "no-go" at this point, explain why and continue with the exercise to confirm your decision.

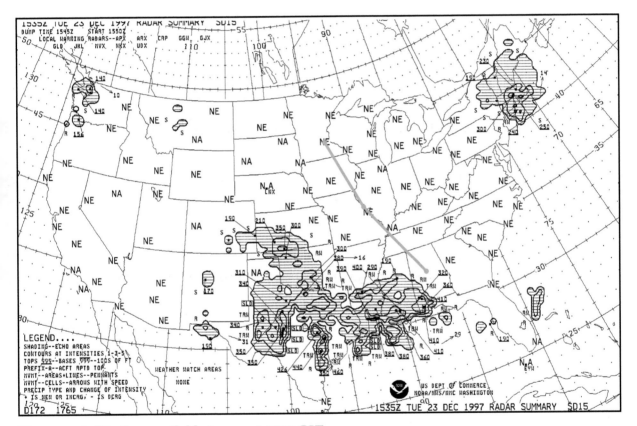

Figure 17-6. Weather available to you at 1000 CST.

TASK 17-6: 1100 CST, DECEMBER 23.

Terminal aerodrome forecasts made during the last hour for terminals on and near the proposed route are given in figure 17-7.

1. What and where are the potentially hazardous weather conditions at the time of your proposed departure and along the track of your flight?

2. Would you modify your flight plan at this point? How?

3. If you elect a "no-go" at this point, explain why and continue with the exercise to confirm your decision.

```
TAF
KBHM 231730Z 231818 08006KT P6SM SCT040 OVC100
      TEMPO 1820 5SM -RA BR OVC040
    FM2000 09008KT 6SM -RA SCT030 OVC080
      TEMPO 2024 4SM -RA OVC030
    FM0000 09010KT 4SM -RA BR OVC030
      TEMPO 0509 2SM TSRA BR OVC015CB
    FM0900 14014G22KT 2SM -RA BR OVC008
      TEMPO 0915 1/2SM +TSRA OVC005CB=


TAF
KMEM 231730Z 231818 13005KT P6SM OVC015
    FM2100 07005KT P6SM OVC035
      TEMPO 2103 4SM -RA
    FM0300 07012KT 3SM -RA BR OVC020
    FM0600 09015KT 2SM RA BR OVC008
    FM1000 25015KT 5SM BR OVC015=


TAF
KSTL 231730Z 231818 VRB05KT P6SM OVC014
    FM0700 07012KT 3SM BR OVC008
      TEMPO 0710 1SM -RA BR OVC004
    FM1000 06015KT 3SM -RA BR OVC004
    FM1500 06010KT 3SM -RA BR OVC004=


TAF
KMSP 231735Z 231818 VRB04KT 4SM BR OVC010
      TEMPO 1821 P6SM
    FM2300 16007KT P6SM OVC015
    FM0300 15006KT P6SM SCT015
    FM1300 20006KT P6SM SCT080=
```

Figure 17-7. Weather available to you at 1100 CST.

TASK 17-7: 1200 CST, DECEMBER 23.

Updated Convective SIGMETs received in the last hour are shown in alphanumeric form in figure 17-8 and as a graphic in figure 17-9.

1. What and where are the potentially hazardous weather conditions at the time of your proposed departure and along the track of your flight?

2. Would you modify your flight plan at this point? How?

3. If you elect a "no-go" at this point, explain why and continue with the exercise to confirm your decision.

```
ZCZC MKCWSTC
WSUS41 KMKC 231755
MKCC WST 231755
CONVECTIVE SIGMET 41C
VALID UNTIL 1955Z
TX
FROM 60E SJT-70ESE DRT
LINE EMBD TS 20 NM WIDE MOV FROM 24030KT. TOPS TO FL350.


CONVECTIVE SIGMET 42C
VALID UNTIL 1955Z
TX
20ESE DRT
ISOL EMBD TS D20 MOV FROM 24030KT. TOPS TO FL300.


CONVECTIVE SIGMET 43C
VALID UNTIL 1955Z
TX
FROM 50WSW SPS-30N DFW-1ON ACT-20E ABI-50WSW SPS
AREA EMBD TS MOV FROM 20035KT. TOPS TO FL350.


CONVECTIVE SIGMET 44C
VALID UNTIL 1955Z
OK TX
FROM 60NW TXK-60ESE AUS-30NE AUS-40ESE ADM-60NW TXK
AREA SEV TS MOV FROM 20035KT. TOPS TO FL430.
HAIL TO 1 IN...WIND GUSTS TO 50 KT POSS.


CONVECTIVE SIGMET 45C
VALID UNTIL 1955Z
TX LA
30W LCH
ISOL EMBD TS D30 MOV FROM 20035KT. TOPS TO FL400.


CONVECTIVE SIGMET 46C
VALID UNTIL 1955Z
LA MS
FROM 30SE JAN-50E MSY-30SW MSY-30N AEX-30SE JAN
AREA EMBD TS MOV FROM 20035KT. TOPS TO FL400.


OUTLOOK VALID 231955-232355
FROM GCK-OSW-MEM-AMG-100W PIE-BRO-60WNW DRT--GCK
COMPLEX WINTER STORM DVLPG ACRS SRN PLNS..TX AND LWR MISS RVR
VLY. MAIN SFC LOW EXP TO DVLP ACRS SERN TX...WITH WRMFNT EWD
THRU NRN GULFMEX AND CDFNT THRU SRN TX. BY 24/06Z...LOW EXP TO
INTSF..MOV TO NWRN LA WITH WRMFNT LIFTING THRU SRN PTNS OF GULF
CST STATES..AS CDFNT SWEEPS ACRS WRN GULFMEX. ISOL TO WDLY SCT
EMBD TS ACT EXP ACRS FAR NRN PTNS OF OUTLOOK AREA... WITH ACT
BECMG MORE NMRS VCY WRMFNT. STG MOIST CONVGC/WAA/ELEVATED
INSTBY ALG/N OF WRMFNT. STG UPR LVL DIFFLUENCE AIDING TS ACT.
WRM SECTOR EXP TO BECM MORE ACT THIS AFTN/EVNG. SCT TO NRMS TS
ACT EXP MOST OF OUTLOOK AREA...FRMG INTO LNS/CLUSTERS. GOOD
THREAT OF SEV TS SERN TX THRU SRN MS. SEE SPC DISCUSSIONS. TS
ACT WILL CONT TO RQR WST ISSUANCES.
```

Figure 17-8. Weather available to you at 1200 CST.

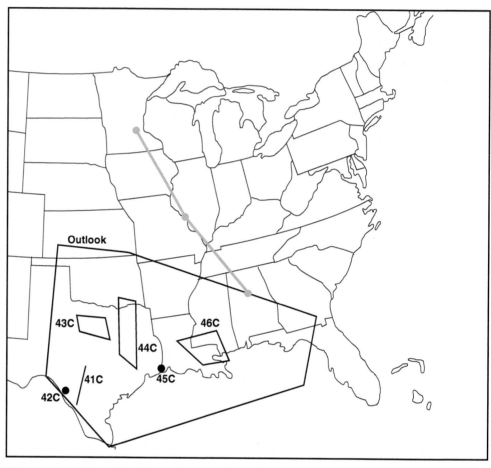

Figure 17-9. Graphic plots of areas described in the convective SIGMETs and outlook given in figure 17-8. Flight track shown in blue.

TASK 17-8: 1230 CST, DECEMBER 23.

It is now about one hour from your proposed departure time. The most recent METARs are obtained for several stations along your planned track. These are listed in figure 17-10.

1. What and where are the potentially hazardous weather conditions at the time of your proposed departure and along the track of your flight?

NAME: _____

DATE: _____ CLASS: _____

2. Would you modify your flight plan at this point? How?

3. If you elect a "no-go" at this point, explain why and continue with the exercise to confirm your decision.

```
KBHM 231350Z 00000KT 7SM FEW140 BKN250 04/03 A3011 RMK SLP197 T00410031=
KBHM 231450Z 18003KT 7SM FEW100 BKN140 OVC250 07/06 A3012 RMK SLP201 T00690063
 55000=
KBHM 231552Z 06005KT 7SM FEW100 OVC140 09/07 A3010 RMK SLP193 T00880068=
KBHM 231650Z 00000KT 8SM FEW110 OVC140 10/07 A3009 RMK SLP190 T00990066=
KBHM 231750Z 35004KT 6SM HZ FEW110 OVC140 09/07 A3008 RMK SLP186 T00930071
 10106 20023 56014=

KMEM 231352Z 36005KT 12SM OVC017 07/05 A3014 RMK SLP207 T00740051=
KMEM 231550Z 09004KT 15SM OVC019 08/05 A3016 RMK SLP214 T00830046=
KMEM 231651Z 13006KT 12SM OVC018 08/05 A3013 RMK SLP204 T00830047=
KMEM 231750Z VRB05KT 12SM OVC017 08/05 A3007 RMK PRESFR SLP183 T00820048 10084
 20066 58024=

KSTL 231353Z 25004KT 6SM BR BKN013 OVC050 02/00 A3015 RMK AO2 SLP219 T00170000=
KSTL 231417Z 26006KT 6SM BR BKN015 OVC050 02/01 A3016 RMK AO2=
KSTL 231453Z 29006KT 7SM BKN015 OVC050 03/01 A3016 RMK AO2 SLP221 T00280006
 51012=
KSTL 231553Z 31007KT 8SM OVC015 03/01 A3016 RMK AO2 SLP222 T00280006=
KSTL 231636Z 29005KT 8SM OVC013 03/01 A3015 RMK AO2=
KSTL 231653Z 29004KT 8SM OVC013 03/01 A3015 RMK AO2 SLP217 T00330006=
KSTL 231753Z 00000KT 8SM OVC015 03/01 A3011 RMK AO2 SLP204 T00330006 10039
 20000 58016=

KMSP 231355Z 23004KT 5SM BR OVC012 M02/M04 A3007 RMK AO2 SLP194 T10221044=
KMSP 231455Z 00000KT 4SM HZ OVC012 M02/M05 A3009 RMK AO2 SLP202 T10221050 52008=
KMSP 231555Z VRB03KT 4SM HZ OVC012 M02/M05 A3009 RMK AO2 SLP201 T10221050=
KMSP 231655Z 23004KT 4SM HZ OVC012 M02/M05 A3008 RMK AO2 SLP197 T10171050=
KMSP 231755Z 16006KT 4SM HZ OVC012 M02/M05 A3006 RMK AO2 SLP189 T10171050 11011
 21022 58011=
```

Figure 17-10. Weather available to you at 1230 CST.

TASK 17-9: 1245 CST, DECEMBER 23.

The final pieces of available information are PIREPs. Figure 17-11 shows the reports that were made in the last 45 minutes. Use the plotting chart in figure 17-12 to identify the locations of the PIREPs.

1. Draw your flight track on figure 17-12.

2. What and where are the potentially hazardous weather conditions at the time of your proposed departure and along the track of your flight?

3. Would you modify your flight plan at this point? How?

4. If you elect a "no-go" at this point, explain why.

NAME: _____

DATE: _____ CLASS: _____

```
STL UA /OV STL/TM 1815/FLUNKN/TP MD80/SK 010 OVC 033/CA=

JBR UUA /OV UJM/TM 1841/FL210-170/TP DC9/TB MOD 180-150/IC SEV RIM
    E/RM ZME=

ALO UA /OV ALO/TM 1830/FLDURD/TP BA31/SK 017 OVC 028=

ANB UA /OV ANB/TM 1841/FL012/TP PA32/SK 012 OVC/RM DURGD=

JBR UA /OV UJM225020/TM 1835/FL210/TP DC9/IC MOD MXD/RM ZME=

ELD UA /OV MEM-SHV/TM 1825/FL040/TP BE35/SK TOPS 035/TA -15/RM ABV
    CLDS HI CI TO EAST OF MISS RVR SCUD LYR LLQ-3M9 OCNL R=

MCW UA /OV MCW180020/TM 1835/FL290/TP F100/TB CONT MDT=

RST UA /OV RST/TM 1827/FL350/TP B767/WV 265038/TB OCNL MDT CHOP/RM
    SMTH FL370-390=

STL UA /OV STL/TM 1830/FLUNKN/TP BA31/SK 021 OVC 033/CA=

MKL UA /OV MKL/TM 1812/FL060/TP JSTA/SK 024 OVC 036/RM HIER LYR
    ABV=

JBR UA /OV ELD030085/TM 1804/FL160/TP DC9/TB LGT-MDT=

COU UA COU/TM 1827/FLDURC/TP PA28/SK OVC 054/CA/IC NEG/RM
    DURGC COU=

MSP UA /OV MSP 090003/TM 1827/FLUNKN/TP B737/SK 022 OVC 028=

STL UA /OV STL-FQF090120/TM 1820/FL390/TP G2/TB LGT CHOP=
```

Figure 17-11. Weather available to you at 1330 CST.

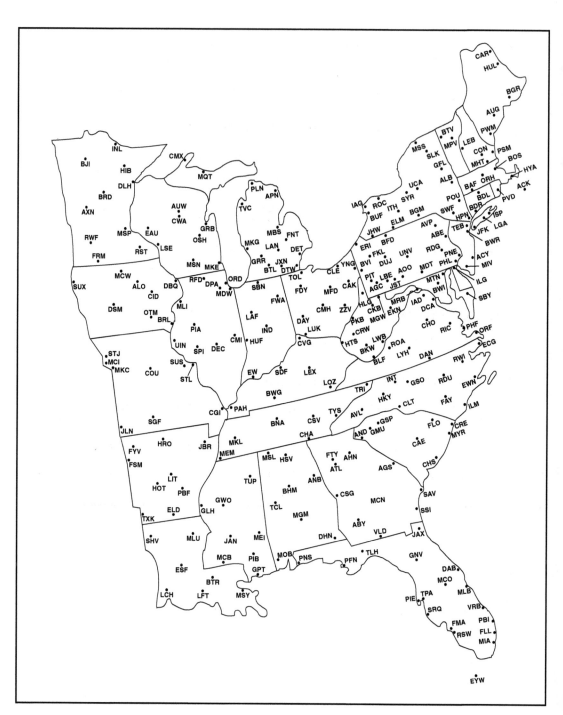

Figure 17-12. PIREP Location Chart.

NAME: _____

DATE: _____ CLASS: _____

TASK 17-10: 1330 CST, DECEMBER 23.

Your departure time has arrived. Answer the following questions.

1. Did you decide to make the flight as originally planned? If so, what led you to make that decision? What are the potential hazards of continuing the flight as planned? How will you confirm these hazards enroute?

2. Did you decide to modify the flight plan? If so, what led you to make the decision to modify the flight plan? What are the potential hazards of continuing with the modified flight plan?

3. Did you decide to cancel the flight? If so, what led you to make the decision to cancel?

CAUTION: The above flight planning scenario was designed as an educational exercise. Data were limited and modified somewhat to give you thoughtful practice in using real-time meteorological data for flight planning. In an actual flight planning situation, you would, of course, use all meteorological information and appropriate, available briefing services.

QUESTIONS

1. Although the flight was conducted in the lower troposphere, the 300 mb chart was useful in your evaluation of conditions. Explain.

2. Write the CST date and time on each weather product in this exercise.

3. Instructor's choice: Repeat the exercise using the same data, but change the route to one of the following:

   MSP to BHM

   BHM to STL

   MSP to STL

4. (Optional) With your instructor's guidance, plan a cross-country flight of similar length with an early afternoon takeoff. Specify the aircraft and pilot's qualifications. If you are a pilot, use your own qualifications. Based on your weather "overview," choose a route with (initially) slightly marginal weather conditions. Do this task in real time; that is, start early and obtain and interpret key information as it becomes available. As opposed to the just-completed Exercise 17, where possible, use color graphics and plotted and interactive text information available from the Aviation Weather Center Website, http://aviationweather.gov/. Document your timeline, data acquisition process, and the development of your final decision.